S * A * C

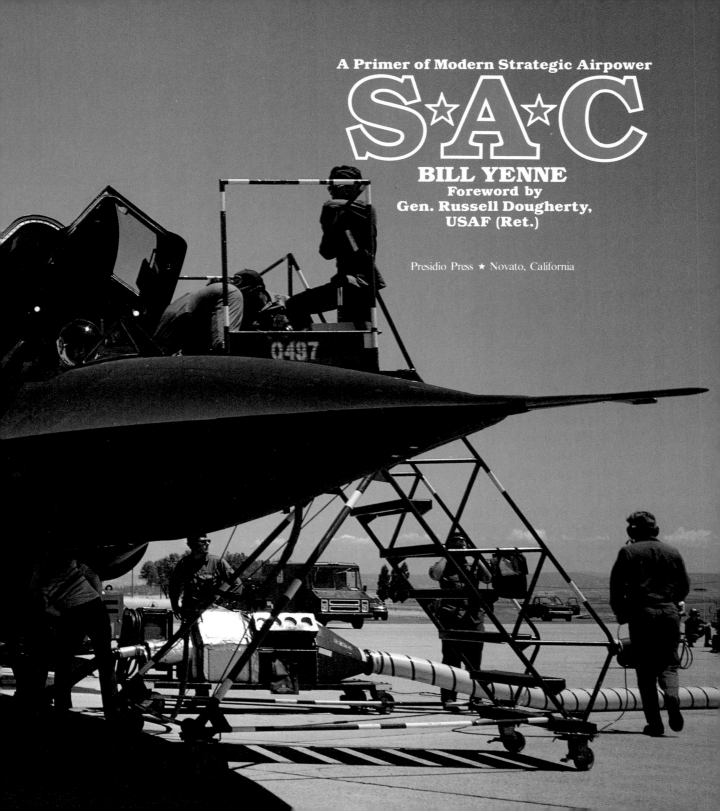

A Primer of Modern Strategic Airpower

S★A★C

BILL YENNE
Foreword by
Gen. Russell Dougherty,
USAF (Ret.)

Presidio Press ★ Novato, California

Published by Presidio Press, 31 Pamaron Way, Novato,
CA 94947

Produced by AGS Books, 576 Sacramento Street,
San Francisco 94111

Library of Congress Cataloging in Publication Data

Yenne, Bill, 1949–
  SAC, a Primer of Modern Strategic Airpower.

  (The Presidio Airpower series)
  1. United States. Air Force. Strategic Air
  Command.
I. Title. II. Title: SAC, a Primer of Modern Strategic
Airpower. III. Series.
UG633.Y46 1985 358.4′2′0973 84-11648
ISBN 0-89141-189-5

Design and Maps by Bill Yenne
Printed by Dai Nippon

Notes on Sources:
Data used in the text and charts in this book was derived
from many official sources including *The Development
of the Strategic Air Command* by J. C. Hopkins and
SAC Tanker Operations in the Southeast Asia War by
Charles K. Hopkins, both published by the Office of the
Historian, Headquarters, Strategic Air Command.
Quotations were derived from *Linebacker II: A View
From the Rock* by Brig. Gen. James R. McCarthy and Lt.
Col. George B. Allison, edited by Col. Robert E. Rayfield,
published under the auspices of the Airpower Research
Institute, Air War College, Maxwell AFB; and *Arms
Control and Disarmament Agreements,* published by the
United States Arms Control Disarmament Agency.

All the photos in this book are Official US Air Force
photos with the following exceptions:
  Author's Collection: 39, 40, 45
  National Air & Space Museum: 38, 43, 46, 50, 122
  US Arms Control & Disarmament Agency: 131, 133
  Photographed by the author (Bill Yenne): front cover
  (except lower left), title page, 8-9, 9, 12-13, 13, 20-21,
  28-29, 29.
  Bill Yenne: 4-5, 72, 75, 92, 105, 111, 113, 117, 119, 125

Front cover: top: A 93d Bomb Wing B-52G about to
touch down at Castle AFB, California;
lower left: Air-Launched Cruise Missiles are mounted on
pylons beneath a B-52's wing;
center: The official SAC insignia was designed by S/Sgt.
R.T. Barnes of the 92d Bomb Wing, at Fairchild AFB,
Washington, in 1951 as a part of a command-wide
competition with 60 entrants. This winning design was
selected by Generals LeMay, Power and Kissner and
officially adopted on January 4, 1952;
lower right: A KC-135 Stratotanker lowers its refueling
boom. SAC operates all of the USAF's tanker fleet.

Back cover: The control center for SAC's global
operations is three stories below SAC Headquarters at
Offutt AFB, Nebraska.

Frontispiece: SAC B-52D heavy bombers over their
target in Southeast Asia.

Title page: An SR-71 Blackbird reconnaissance aircraft is
prepared for take off from Beale AFB. SAC, the only
user of SR-71s, home-bases all of its Blackbirds at Beale.

Opposite page: In late 1957 as part of a reenlistment
program, a sign was to be erected at SAC Headquarters
with the slogan "Maintaining Peace is our Profession".
There wasn't enough room, so the first word was
omitted. Colonel Charles Van Vliet, Eighth Air Force
director of information saw the temporary sign on a visit
to Offutt and had the slogan used on a sign back at
Eighth Air Force Headquarters, then at Westover AFB
Massachusetts. Other Eighth Air Force bases picked up
the slogan and soon it was being quoted in the press. By
the end of 1958, "Peace is our Profession" was adopted
by SAC Headquarters as the official SAC slogan.

Page vi: A B-52G armed with Air Launched Cruise
Missiles snuggles up to a KC-135 for refueling.

Page 1; General Russell E. Dougherty as Commander in
Chief, Strategic Air Command.

Contents

Foreword   1

Part I: A Portrait of SAC
1   War, Deterrence, and the Triad   3
2   SAC Central   25
3   Strategic Reconnaissance   31

Part II: Strategic Airpower Before SAC
4   Origins of Strategic Airpower   37
5   Strategic Air Power in Europe   42
6   Strategic Air Offensive in the Pacific   52

Part III: SAC's Formative Years
7   The Creation of SAC   57
8   LeMay Comes Aboard   63
9   SAC in Korea   66
10   The Big Stick   63
11   The Changing of the Guard   73
12   SAC Missile Forces   80

Part IV: SAC in Southeast Asia
13   Dreaming of a "Sub-limited War"   85
14   SAC Goes to War   86

15   Expanding SAC Tanker Operations   92
16   Arc Light Rolls On   96
17   "Press On"   100
18   Linebacker II   101

Part V: SAC in an Uncertain World
19   The Other Strategic Air Commands   121
20   Strategic Arms Control   128
Glossary   136
Acknowledgements   138

Foreword

Many months ago Bill Yenne discussed with me his intention to write a comprehensive book on the Strategic Air Command—its conceptual roots and principal tenets, its ancestral organizations, and its evolution from post–World War II founding to its present maturity as a major combatant command of the United States. My initial reaction was one of skepticism; there was simply too much to tell, and it just would not fit into a single writing.

This book proves me wrong. Bill Yenne has done all the things that he set out to do and done them well. The SAC story is told in its many dimensions in a comprehensive, interesting format without compromising essential facts or pertinent situations. Essential background and details are supplied in a fashion that will serve to educate the student seeking initial knowledge as well as assist the critical researcher seeking to expand the scope of his analysis. This book will complement, equally, the libraries of thoughtful private citizens and the serious stacks of our professional War College libraries.

Mr. Yenne has gone well beyond the mere assimilation of events over dates and places. He has given us valuable perspectives on the relationship of emerging aerospace thought and technology as they relate to shaping events or responding to them. All too often we tend to overlook (or, even worse, to ignore) the importance of integrating our principal military strengths and technologies into a purposeful national design. Evolution of strategic aerospace power has often been achieved only after initial mistakes or inept applications; too much of its history has been written as happenstance. All this is explored in this book. There have been several dramatic instances in which our nation properly recognized and exploited the vital political/military aspects of its strategic military strengths— signal among them was the creation of Strategic Air Command. There have been equally dramatic instances in which we failed to do so, such as the fateful decision not to attack strategic targets in North Vietnam early in the 1960s.

These valuable lessons are well set out here. They can serve as prologue for the effective handling of the ever more hazardous complexities of the future. Mr. Yenne has done all of us a favor by analyzing both the proper use and the abuse of our strategic strengths. Would that we will understand and profit from these valuable insights while we enjoy this interesting account of the development of the United States Air Force's Strategic Air Command.

General Russell E. Dougherty, USAF (Ret.)
Commander, Strategic Air Command (1974-1977)
Executive Director, Air Force Association

Part I
A Portrait of SAC

1 War, Deterrence, and the Triad

Somewhere up on the northern tier of the United States a B–52 shrieks to life, its belly filled with air-launched cruise missiles, its flight deck filled with men who know the mission plan, the never-ending airborne alert deterrent mission plan, but have no memory of the men of their fathers' generation who sat at these same controls and flew the same mission with the old Mk–28 gravity-fall nuclear bombs tucked into the bay.

Somewhere far beneath the vast plains of the central United States, parched and dusty under a relentless sun or whipped by a howling blizzard, two men, oblivious to the outside world behind steel and concrete doors, sit at electronic consoles maintained in prime operating condition for decades but never in all that time used for their designated purpose.

Somewhere in Geneva, Switzerland, a man about the same age as the others, educated in political science, his uniform a pinstripe suit, not air force blue, takes a last gulp of thick French coffee, places a sheaf of papers back in his briefcase and dashes toward the car that will take him and his co-workers to another round of arms

Left: The B-1, archetypical SAC bomber for the nineties.

control talks, which have been going round and round since before he even knew what they were.

Somewhere in the trackless wastes of Siberia, in a drafty radar shack, a fourth man, who will never know or understand the others, lights another foul-smelling Armenian cigarette and stares at the circular screen before him, its images like green popcorn beneath a thick sheet of plate glass, as he and those before him have done for years. He squints at the ghostly images. Are they massing B–52s? a Korean airliner? a *Soviet* airliner? a flock of geese on their way south across the taiga? His training has taught him to read these floating specters, and today he reads no threat. Another day has passed and a comforting, flat black darkness of night descended over a world spared for one more day the horror of nuclear annihilation.

The world has lived with nuclear weapons since 1945, and since 1949 it has seen the peace kept by an uneasy truce between two powerful and opposing nations with nuclear capability. Nuclear weapons were first developed to win a war four decades ago, and they have not been used in anger since. Their own awesome destructive power has deterred their use. The old adage "If you want peace, prepare for war" is more true than ever in the age of thermonuclear weapons. The superpower nuclear arsenals exist to convince the other side that to risk a nuclear attack is to invite destruction.

When the Strategic Air Command was born, its role was to prepare to conduct strategic air

Strategic Air Command

First Strategic Aerospace Division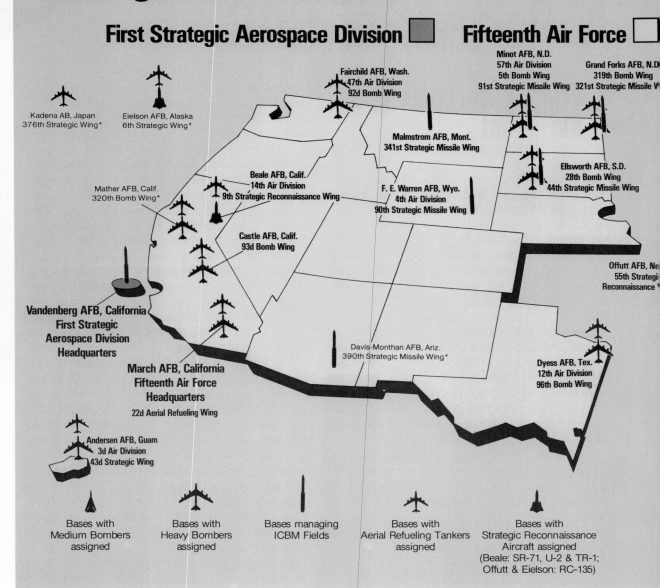

Fifteenth Air Force

Kadena AB, Japan
376th Strategic Wing*

Eielson AFB, Alaska
6th Strategic Wing*

Fairchild AFB, Wash.
47th Air Division
92d Bomb Wing

Minot AFB, N.D.
57th Air Division
5th Bomb Wing
91st Strategic Missile Wing

Grand Forks AFB, N.D.
319th Bomb Wing
321st Strategic Missile W

Malmstrom AFB, Mont.
341st Strategic Missile Wing

Ellsworth AFB, S.D.
28th Bomb Wing
44th Strategic Missile Wing

Beale AFB, Calif.
14th Air Division
9th Strategic Reconnaissance Wing

F. E. Warren AFB, Wyo.
4th Air Division
90th Strategic Missile Wing

Mather AFB, Calif.
320th Bomb Wing*

Castle AFB, Calif.
93d Bomb Wing

Offutt AFB, Ne
55th Strategi
Reconnaissance

Vandenberg AFB, California
First Strategic
Aerospace Division
Headquarters

March AFB, California
Fifteenth Air Force
Headquarters
22d Aerial Refueling Wing

Davis-Monthan AFB, Ariz.
390th Strategic Missile Wing*

Dyess AFB, Tex.
12th Air Division
96th Bomb Wing

Andersen AFB, Guam
3d Air Division
43d Strategic Wing

Bases with
Medium Bombers
assigned

Bases with
Heavy Bombers
assigned

Bases managing
ICBM Fields

Bases with
Aerial Refueling Tankers
assigned

Bases with
Strategic Reconnaissance
Aircraft assigned
(Beale: SR-71, U-2 & TR-1;
Offutt & Eielson: RC-135)

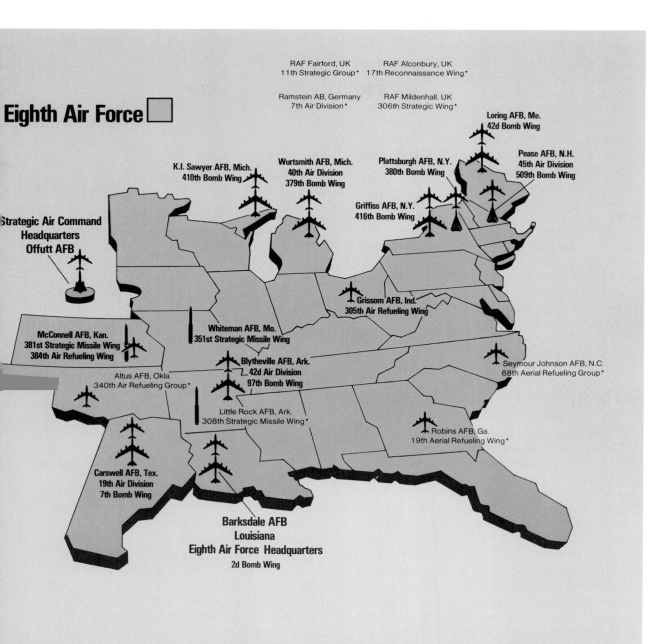

Eighth Air Force

RAF Fairford, UK
11th Strategic Group*

RAF Alconbury, UK
17th Reconnaissance Wing*

Ramstein AB, Germany
7th Air Division*

RAF Mildenhall, UK
306th Strategic Wing*

Loring AFB, Me.
42d Bomb Wing

Pease AFB, N.H.
45th Air Division
509th Bomb Wing

K.I. Sawyer AFB, Mich.
410th Bomb Wing

Wurtsmith AFB, Mich.
40th Air Division
379th Bomb Wing

Plattsburgh AFB, N.Y.
380th Bomb Wing

Griffiss AFB, N.Y.
416th Bomb Wing

Strategic Air Command
Headquarters
Offutt AFB

Grissom AFB, Ind.
305th Air Refueling Wing

McConnell AFB, Kan.
381st Strategic Missile Wing
384th Air Refueling Wing

Whiteman AFB, Mo.
351st Strategic Missile Wing

Seymour Johnson AFB, N.C.
68th Aerial Refueling Group*

Altus AFB, Okla.
340th Air Refueling Group*

Blytheville AFB, Ark.
42d Air Division
97th Bomb Wing

Little Rock AFB, Ark.
308th Strategic Missile Wing*

Robins AFB, Ga.
19th Aerial Refueling Wing*

Carswell AFB, Tex.
19th Air Division
7th Bomb Wing

Barksdale AFB
Louisiana
Eighth Air Force Headquarters

2d Bomb Wing

*Bases indicated in small type are non-SAC bases with SAC units assigned.

5

warfare. The American arsenal is built on a three-legged stool known as the strategic Triad, the use of three distinctly different weapons systems, each with its own characteristics of effectiveness and survivability. Two of the three legs of the Triad (manned bombers and ICBMs—intercontinental ballistic missiles) are under the command control of the Strategic Air Command, and the third (submarine-launched ballistic missiles—SLBMs) is controlled by the U.S. Navy.

SAC's primary role is to act as the U.S. Air Force's long-range strategic strike force, maintaining and controlling strategic bombers and missiles for immediate reaction in time of nuclear war, but SAC also maintains two fleets of aircraft for ancillary functions. First, there is the fleet of over six hundred Boeing KC–135 Stratotankers, and recently, nearly fifty McDonnell Douglas KC–10 Extenders, aerial refueling tankers that serve the aerial refueling needs of the entire U.S. Air Force. Second is a fleet of highly secret high-performance reconnaissance aircraft.

SAC Bombers

The manned bomber is the oldest and central element of strategic airpower and of SAC's arsenal since it was formed in 1946. The B–52 Stratofortress, now into its third decade of service, is the mainstay of the SAC bomber fleet. The first gleaming silver B–52s joined SAC in 1955, and the last one rolled off Boeing's Wichita assembly line in 1963. Today the big bomber is neither gleaming nor silver, but it is perhaps all the more awesome for its dark, scuffed camouflage paint scheme.

Back on the sun-bleached, skid-streaked tarmac on America's northern tier, the venerable old B–52s begin to roll. As they taxi toward the takeoff point, the big hulking planes crowd together into a slow-moving line known to the crews

as the "elephant walk." The noise is deafening. Noise control is simply not an issue at a remote SAC base the way it is at a commercial airport, and anyway, the B–52s were built before all this sissy noise-damping technology was heard of. These thundering beasts are the only aircraft ever to go into operational service with *eight* jet engines, double the number of engines you'll see on any airplane at any airport.

The first bell has yet to ring at the base grammar school, but out here on the plains the horizon is low and the sun has been baking the runway for several hours. Even with the air temperature creeping toward the nineties, the heat

waves from the engine blast of the lead plane have turned it into a swirling indistinguishable mass.

Inside the crowded cockpit, sweat is beginning to trickle down the side of the pilot's head where the helmet creases his forehead. Though most of the crew are in their twenties, too young to have seen these planes when they were new, the pilot is a major in his forties who has seen it all. His gloved hand has spread across this trembling mass of eight throttles maybe hundreds of times. The subtleties have changed over the years, but the mission plan remains the same. As he pushes those eight levers forward, send-ing the old plane screaming down the runway like an angry dragon, he is not sure—indeed, no one is sure—whether today will be the day the word will come that will cause him to ask the navigator to give him a heading for some un-pronounceable Tartar city wrapped deep in the hostile airspace of Soviet Russia.

As the eight huge tires that carried the plane on its skyward crawl slam back into the wheel-wells, the pilot and the copilot glance around a cockpit that earlier occupants of their seats would not recognize. Throughout the decade and a half

following the war in Southeast Asia, the modifications made to the B–52G and H, the newest and only remaining B–52 models, have virtually turned them into new airplanes. The centerpiece of the new cockpit is the ethereal green glow of a pair of video display terminals that permit the plane to be flown under visibility conditions that include dark of night or dense fog. The pilot and copilot can fly the plane by watching these screens, which use the electro-optical viewing system (EVS). The EVS consists of a pair of movable cameras located in the chin of the air-

craft, one a Westinghouse AVQ–22 low-light television (LLTV) camera and the other a Hughes AAQ–6 forward-locking infrared sensor (FLIR). The pilot can fly the aircraft under any visibility conditions by keeping his eyes on one of two video display terminals in the cockpit, which give him an image of the outside world as though it were illuminated by daylight and superimpose operational data such as speed, altitude, time to go on the mission, and so forth, over a television picture of the terrain outside. The modifications have also involved a greatly upgraded avionics package, which includes advanced capability terrain-avoidance radar (ACR) allowing the big aircraft to fly only 300 feet off the ground. The B–52 was originally designed as a high-altitude bomber, but a mission flown against modern air defenses would probably have to be flown at low altitude, below enemy radar.

The General Dynamics FB–111 "Aardvark" is SAC's medium-range strategic bomber. Converted from the basic variable-geometry F–111 fighter and introduced in 1969, the FB–111 is capable of supersonic flight at various altitudes,

9

Above: An FB–111 medium bomber loaded for bear.

including sea level. The variable-geometry characteristics of the Aardvark permit in-flight changes in the degree of wing sweep to permit stable, efficient performance throughout the plane's speed spectrum. As SAC points out, "the variable-sweep wing, in effect, enables the pilot to redesign his aircraft in flight." Fully extended to 16 degrees of sweep, the wing creates a maximum span of surface area for maximum lift, permitting short takeoffs and landings. At supersonic speeds, the wings can be swept back to 72.5 degrees, reducing drag. Weapons pylons mounted on the wings are designed to swivel as the wings change position. The wing pylons and the internal bomb bay can accommodate 31,500 pounds of conventional bombs, or six nuclear bombs.

Comparisons are often made between the FB–111 and the Convair B–58 of the 1960s, SAC's first supersonic bomber. First of all, whereas the B–58 was designed as a strategic bomber, the FB–111 evolved from a tactical fighter, growing out of the tactical fighter experimental (TFX) program of the mid-sixties. Despite its origins, the FB–111 is three quarters the length of the B–58 and has a *maximum* bomb weight capac-

ity nearly 40 percent greater than the earlier bomber's normal payload. In terms of speed, the two Pratt & Whitney TF–30–P–7 turbofans push the FB–111 to Mach 2.5, whereas the four General Electric J–79–5 turbojets of the B–58 permitted little more than Mach 2, though, for practical purposes, the external weapons pod of the B–58 was aerodynamically much cleaner than the underwing pylons of the FB–111. The range of neither plane approaches that of the larger B–52 or the later B–1, which is a factor that puts them both in the medium bomber class. The B–58 could range 5,125 miles without external fuel versus 3,165 miles for the FB–111 under similar conditions.

Products of the technology of two different eras, the two aircraft, built by essentially the same company (Convair became a division of General Dynamics), have come to fulfill the same role for SAC. Two aspects of this advancing technology that make the FB–111 superior to the earlier strategic bomber are its ability to carry six AGM–69 SRAM (short-range attack missiles) as an alternative to a conventional or nuclear bomb load

Above: One of the four prototype B-1As in SAC markings.

and its unique terrain following radar (TFR). The TFR, like the terrain avoidance radar in the B-52, permits the FB-111 to fly at very low altitude (below enemy radar) and very high speed over irregular terrain without colliding with ground features such as hills and buildings. In Southeast Asia, where the FB-111 was first used, it was this ability to arrive over the target before its own sound and without radar warning that earned it the nickname "Whispering Death."

The most controversial combat aircraft of recent times is the Rockwell (incorporating North American Aviation) B-1. It was originally conceived in the late sixties under the advanced manned strategic aircraft (AMSA) program as the strategic bomber that was to replace the B-52 by 1980. The B-1 first flew in December 1974 and first exceeded Mach 2 in April 1976. It was planned that two hundred fifty B-1s would be produced and go into service with SAC by the mid-eighties, but congressional budget opposition proved to be an early thorn in the big bird's smooth white skin. With the election in 1976 of President Jimmy Carter, who was known to cast

a wary eye on defense spending, the B-1 program was clearly in trouble. In June 1977 the Carter administration announced that the B-1 would be canceled and that production would stop with the fourth prototype, which would first fly in January 1979. In the words of the defense department's fiscal year 1980 report: "We are continuing the testing of the B-1 bomber design so that the technical base will be available in the *very unlikely* [italics added] event that, because alternative strategic systems run into difficulty, we decide to reconsider B-1 deployment. This program will evaluate the penetration effectiveness of the B-1, provide information on current and future applications of the defensive avionics and engine design, and measure the B-1's resistance to nuclear effects."

It seemed as though another successor to the B-52, like the earlier B-70, would be snatched from life at the prototype stage to serve as a research aircraft and never, as intended, with SAC operational units. Jimmy Carter was, however, replaced in 1981 by Ronald Reagan, whose administration was more favorably disposed to the idea of replacing obsolete weapons systems. By February 1981, charged with the goal

of developing another successor to the B–52, the U.S. Air Force reported to Congress that "the current bomber program centers on an aggressive evaluation program whose goal will lead to a selection of a candidate [for] multirole bomber, or Long-Range Combat Aircraft (LRCA), as we have called it. Near-term candidates include B–1 variants, a stretched version of the FB–111, and a new design based on currently available technology. Longer-term alternatives address advanced-technology design. We believe a mid-1980s Initial Operational Capability (IOC) of 15

Above: A B-1 in desert camouflage colors prepares for take off.

Left: A black-bellied B-52D of the 3d Air Division photographed by the author at Andersen AFB, Guam in 1979. B-52s flew hundreds of combat missions from here between 1965 and 1973.

aircraft is feasible for either B–1 or FB–111B/C candidates. It is estimated that a B–1 variant would be able to meet an IOC approximately 56–60 months from go-ahead, with final delivery by 1989 based on a buy of 180 aircraft. The FB–111B/C is estimated to meet an IOC about 44–

54 months from go-ahead, with final delivery by 1987 based on a buy of 150 aircraft. Although FB–111B/C IOC occurs earlier, the B–1 variant would have a considerably greater range and weapons lead. The Air Force LRCA program combines funding from the previous Cruise Missile Carrier Aircraft, Strategic Bomber Enhancement, and Bomber Penetration Evaluation programs with that appropriated by Congress for Fiscal Year 1981.''

By May 1981 the need for the LRCA to be a long-range strategic bomber ruled out an aircraft based on the medium-range FB–111. Furthermore the leadtime needed to develop an all-new LRCA design would mean that the resulting LRCA might not come on line before the B–52 had to be phased out. Thus the B–1, still undergoing prototype testing, was the right plane at the right time. On October 2, 1981, the Reagan administration announced that an advanced version of the B–1, designated B–1B, would be procured as SAC's next strategic bomber. One hundred B–1Bs would be delivered beginning in 1985 with a unit cost (in 1981 dollars) of just under $200 million.

The B–1B would differ in a number of important ways from the four B–1As that already had been delivered. Both versions had variable-sweep wings to permit short takeoffs and landings as well as a high-speed pass over the target, but whereas the speed of the B–1A was rated at, and tested at, speeds in excess of Mach 2, the B–1B would be rated at less than Mach 1, in the "high subsonic" range. The "radar signature," or the image of the B–1A on a radar scope, was designed to be as small as one tenth that of the B–52, whereas the radar signature of the B–1B (which is almost exactly the same size as the B–1A) is reported to be, in turn, as small as one tenth that of the B–1A, because of redesigned engine intakes and more radar absorbent surface material. The length of the B–1B is 147 feet 2.5 inches, against 150 feet 2.5 inches for the B–1A and 160 feet 11 inches for the B–52. The wingspan of both B–1s is 136 feet 8.5 inches fully spread and 78 feet 2.5 inches fully swept, versus 185 feet for the B–52, so a radar signature one or two percent of the B–52 would be a significant aid to the B–1B in its mission of penetrating enemy air space.

To further aid in penetration, the B–1B is equipped with a greatly updated offensive avionics system (OAS), ALQ–153 pulse-Doppler tail warning radar, ALQ–161 radio frequency jamming system, and a Westinghouse multifunction radar, that will provide automatic terrain following down to 200 feet and precise navigation functions. The B–1B, which will weigh 238.5 tons, 41 tons more than the B–1A, will also have a much greater weapons-carrying capacity. The B–1B will be able to carry 62.5 tons of ordnance versus 57.5 for the B–1A and 27 tons for the B–52. In addition, the B–1B will be able to carry AGM–86 cruise missiles (ALCMs), a capacity that the newer B–52s have but that the B–1A did not. The B–1B's bomb bay will contain a rotary launcher that will accommodate up to twenty-four nuclear bombs or SRAMs, or eight ALCMs. Another fourteen ALCMs or SRAMs can also be carried on underwing pylons. In a conventional mode, the B–1 can carry up to eighty-four gravity-fall high explosive bombs in its bomb bay and up to another forty-four underwing.

Two of the earlier B–1As were converted to flight-test the upgraded B–1B systems, with the testing begun during the summer of 1983 and the first delivery of an all-new "true" B–1B in December 1984. The first SAC unit to become operational with the B–1B will be the 96th Bomb Wing at Dyess AFB near Abilene, Texas, with sixteen of the new planes to be in service by the summer of 1985.

Another new bird is being developed for the SAC arsenal—a strange and mysterious aircraft first heard about in 1980 just before the presidential election. Jimmy Carter, the Democratic incumbent, was running behind the Republican challenger Ronald Reagan in the polls. The reasons had a lot to do with his lack of support for national defense—what President Theodore Roosevelt would have called the "big stick." Carter had presided over a small decline in military manpower and had canceled the B–1, but the issue was more of morale and attitude than actual tanks-and-planes military power. The big issue in the campaign was the seizing by surrogates of the Iranian government of the American embassy in Tehran and the brutal imprisonment of fifty-three American diplomats and

embassy personnel. Carter had threatened but had made no use of American power to respond to what was, in fact, an act of war by Iran. By his inaction, Carter had injured American prestige in the world, and it is felt by many that his lack of decisive response gave tacit approval to the subsequent Soviet invasion of Afghanistan.

All of this led to Carter's being abandoned in the polls by conservative and middle-of-the-road American voters. In late summer of 1980, with the Americans still held hostage in Iran and the elections staring him in the face, Carter let slip to the news media that his administration was working on a super-secret bomber that was invisible to radar. The bomber was called Stealth, and the leak was intended to show that Carter was secretly not as antidefense as he seemed. The ploy did not work. Those who would have been impressed by the news were shocked at such a closely guarded secret being disclosed during an election campaign. On November 4, Jimmy Carter lost his bid for re-election.

Little more was heard about this Stealth bomber. Probably more was learned from the original news leak than has been heard since, but certain clarifications have caused this strange new aircraft to come into clearer focus. First of all, the project predated the Carter administration, and second, the term *Stealth* describes the technology of reducing an aircraft's radar signature rather than a specific type of aircraft. Radar

responds to sharp angles on objects, so aircraft that are smoother and have rounded corners would have a smaller radar signature. Certain types of surfaces and paints absorb radar waves just as acoustical ceiling tiles absorb sound waves. A lot of these and other elements of stealth technology have been used on aircraft since the seventies and helped to reduce the radar signature of the B-1B.

So, with all of that, is there *really* a top secret Stealth bomber? The answer is yes, but very little is known about this aircraft program, which is officially known as the advanced technology bomber (ATB). The program came up in the summer of 1981 when the decision was being made as to whether to build the B-1B or allow the ATB to replace the B-52. The decision was made at that time to go ahead with both programs. The B-1B would be filling out SAC wings in the late eighties, whereas the ATB would not be operational until the mid-nineties. The idea was that the B-52 would become a second-line strategic bomber to the B-1B by 1990, with the B-1B becoming a second-line strategic bomber to the ATB around the turn of the century, when the latter would be fully operational. The B-52, at least the B-52H, would remain in service until a sizable number of ATBs were in SAC wings. By 1983, the Air Force was moving ahead on flight-testing this strange aircraft that had yet to be seen or photographed in public, and the plan was for 125 of them to be in SAC service ten years later. By early 1984 some of the secrecy had been peeled away, as the trade journal *Aviation Week* began openly to make references to the Stealth bomber as being a "flying wing" type aircraft built by Northrop. In the late forties Northrop had produced a series of flying wing bombers for the Air Force under the service designations B–35 and B–49. These flying wings had been rejected in favor of the B–36 and B–47, but it now seemed as though the flying wing design with its smooth contour and few angles was at last vindicated.

SAC's manned strategic bombers are outfitted with weapons systems that have rendered the old gravity-fall weapons obsolete. To enhance the effectiveness of the SAC bomber fleet, the Air Force has contracted with Boeing Aerospace for the development of ballistic missiles that can be carried by bombers and launched in midair, before the plane encounters enemy defenses.

The first of SAC's air-launched missiles were the Boeing short-range attack missiles (SRAMs), deployed in 1972. The 14-foot SRAM was originally designed to aid bombers in penetration of enemy air defenses by destroying such targets as surface-to-air missile (SAM) sites. For this reason, the range is limited to one hundred miles, but the nuclear warhead has the same megatonnage rating as that of the Minuteman ICBM. The SRAM, which has a maximum speed of Mach 2.5, can be carried on underwing pylons of the FB–111, B–52, or B–1 as well as on the internal rotary launchers in the B–52 and B–1B.

Boeing's AGM–86 air-launched cruise missile (ALCM), first deployed in 1982, though subsonic and hence slower than the SRAM, can deliver a nuclear warhead over a range of fifteen hundred miles. The mission of the ALCM, unlike that of the SRAM, is to strike strategic targets. The ALCM, in effect, turns each bomber into a dozen bombers because the missiles, when released, can dive to earth-hugging altitude and "cruise" individually using their terrain-matching guidance system to separate targets a thousand miles apart, striking them with pinpoint precision. This characteristic of the ALCM allows the carrier aircraft to "stand off" outside the range of enemy defenses, release its weapons, and leave the area without putting itself to the kind of risk incurred by flying to the target and dropping bombs. Meanwhile, on the ground, the enemy must chase a raft of small hard-to-follow targets rather than a single bomber, thus complicating defense. Like the SRAM, the ALCM can be carried internally or externally aboard B–52s and B–1Bs.

ICBMs

As the big B–52s become just a smudge of black exhaust on the horizon and then disappear into the thin upper atmosphere, another, completely different SAC airman is going to work. In lonely, remote places all across the plains that stretch almost endlessly from Montana down to Arkansas and over to Arizona, men in Chevy pickup trucks rattle through gates in chain link fences and creak to a stop near heavily guarded, odd-looking concrete structures. This is the changing of the guard at the second leg of the strategic Triad. This solemn, monotonous ritual has been going on for more than two decades; the odd irony is that this crew goes to its job site so that its presence will prevent its ever having to do its real work.

These airmen will never fly and will not even see the sky during their duty shift. They disappear through small, round trapdoors and descend long ladders into another world—the world of SAC's ICBM fleet, a self-contained underground warren of passageways and bunkers clustered around a ten-story elevator shaft containing a gleaming white projectile. They call them "birds," probably because they are Air Force men and Air Force men have always called the ships they controlled birds, but they are anything but birdlike. They are more like enormous, milky white icicles connected to the walls of their caves by a web of thin, black umbilical cords. These cold and deadly stalagmites have rested in the climate-controlled stillness of their manmade caverns presided over by several generations of doting human servants without ever being cranked up and caused to leap skyward.

It could happen today, though. It could have happened on November 7, 1973, or July 9, 1981, or any other random date. It came very close in October 1962, during the Cuban missile crisis, and several times since. But it didn't happen. The fact that the birds at over a thousand sites have not flown for the men of the more than twenty thousand shifts that each has seen come and go is no guarantee that it won't happen today. Or maybe it is.

Each shift, for all these thousands of shifts, two men have gone to the control room ready to launch their unbirdlike machines, only to clock out without having pushed the "button." The ICBM control room "button" of the popular vernacular is not really a button at all, but rather a pair of ignition switches located on a pair of identical consoles at opposite ends of the room. As part of the maze of safety features built into this deadly game, the missiles cannot be launched without the entire launch procedure being followed precisely and simultaneously by two operators at the two consoles, which are located more than arm's length apart so that one person cannot go through the launch sequence

Right: An MGM-118 Peacekeeper ICBM hurtles skyward from Vandenberg AFB. Originally known as MX, it was the object of intense controversy in the late seventies.

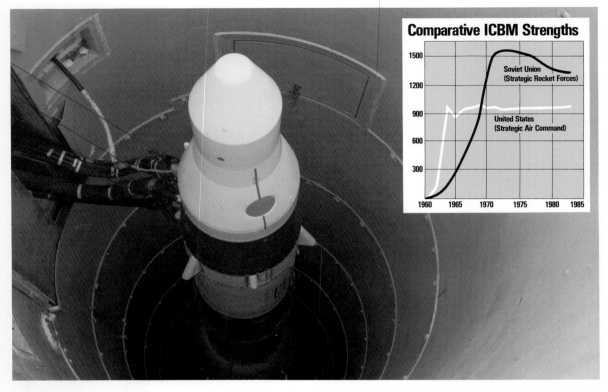

Comparative ICBM Strengths

Soviet Union
(Strategic Rocket Forces)

United States
(Strategic Air Command)

by himself. The sequence begins with the pair of keys issued to the two controllers at the start of each shift; the keys unlock the console and permit the controllers to begin to start the huge engines of the twin ICBMs under their control. The sequence could end in a quiet chill, with the bird flown, the huge cave empty, and the operators waiting speechless in their control rooms for the what-comes-next that no one has yet experienced.

The largest and oldest of SAC's current arsenal of ICBMs is the Martin LGM–25 Titan II. The huge Titan II, 103 feet long, has been in service for two decades, with the last forty-eight of them scheduled to be retired by 1987. The Titan II is a two-stage liquid-fuel ICBM with a range of over five thousand miles and a speed

Above: A Minuteman ICBM in its silo, umbilical cords attached.

of 15,000 mph, allowing it to put its single 9-megaton thermonuclear warhead on target in twenty minutes.

The solid-fuel Boeing LGM–30 Minuteman ICBM first went on alert in SAC in October 1962. Deployed in fields of hardened underground concrete silos, the first was quickly built up to a deployment level of a thousand by April 1967, where it remains today. The 59 foot 10 inch Minuteman is smaller, lighter, and was less expensive than the earlier Titan but has the same speed and a range of up to seven thousand miles. The earlier Minuteman I was replaced by the Minuteman II (LGM–30F) beginning in 1965, and these were augmented by the Minuteman III

(LGM–30G) beginning in June 1970, with the earlier missiles being deactivated to keep the force level at one thousand missiles. Currently there are four hundred fifty Minuteman IIs and five hundred fifty Minuteman IIIs, the latter providing for incorporation of multiple independently targetable reentry vehicles (MIRVs), which means that each Minuteman III has three 175–340-kiloton warheads, each of which can be directed to a different target.

In the late seventies the U.S. Air Force began to study the development of a new ICBM, which was given the interim designation MX (missile, experimental). This missile, now officially designated MGM–118A and code-named Peacekeeper, is still known popularly as MX. The MGM–118A is 71 feet long in four stages, and whereas the MIRVed Minuteman III had three warheads, the MIRVed Peacekeeper has ten 350-kiloton warheads in General Electric Mark 12A reentry vehicles, for a total "throw-weight" of almost four tons. Though the design of the MX has remained fairly constant over its development period, how it will be based has been a subject of great controversy since it was first brought before Congress during the Carter administration. Given the overwhelming lead the Soviet Union had taken in the development of ICBMs, the Carter administration, to its credit, had decided to develop a successor to the Minuteman that would match the multiple-warhead Soviet SS–19 (Soviet designation RS–18) ICBM that was first deployed in 1974.

The basing problem as then perceived worked from the premise that the stationary silos then in use for Minuteman had become vulnerable to a Soviet first strike. If the Russians knew where the missiles were—and they do—each could be targeted and destroyed in a first-strike scenario.

Right: The massive Martin LGM-25 Titan ICBM, seen here with SAC shield and USAF insignia, was SAC's largest missile. The last Titan will have been scrapped by 1987.

To solve this problem, the Carter administration developed what came to be called the racetrack system of basing the MX. Under this scheme, an enormous system of tracks would be built under hundreds of acres of Utah and Nevada desert. The missiles would be randomly moved through these subsurface tunnels so that it would never be clear where the missiles were on the track and the Russians would have to expend several hundred warheads in a first strike and still not be quite sure that they had destroyed all the MX missiles. The incredible expense required by this plan, plus opposition from cattlemen, with whom such a system would have to compete for necessary and scarce water, led the administration to examine other basing modes. Eventually the idea evolved of building a large number of shelters from which the MX *could* be launched, and then moving the missiles from shelter to shelter, like the peas in a shell game, so that the Soviet surveillance satellites in space and ground observers cruising the back roads of Utah in station wagons would never be quite sure which shelter contained a missile. This idea, called the multiple protective shelter (MPS) basing mode, was not well received by the incoming Reagan administration who, though not rejecting the mode out of hand, decided to go back to the drawing board for a possible alternative.

By June 1981 Congress prohibited the spending of $357 million that had been earmarked for MPS construction until the administration decided whether it was going to proceed with MPS or not. Meanwhile, several other proposals were starting to surface. Among them was the logical and cost-effective suggestion of placing the more modern ten-MIRV MX in existing Minuteman silos

Right: A young lieutenant sits at the control panel of a Minuteman silo. Each control center controls its own missiles as well as those of another center if that one should become disabled. This training silo is typical of silos across the nation's midsection that keep the peace through retaliatory potential.

and developing a smaller, more mobile ICBM and some sort of ballistic missile defense (BMD) system. Reagan administration Secretary of Defense Caspar Weinberger concurrently favored development of an airmobile system whereby the MX would be carried by giant C–5 transports (whose cargo hold is many times larger than a bomber's bomb bay). The MX could be dropped by parachute and ignited in midair. Senator John Tower of Texas (chairman of the powerful Senate Armed Services Committee) pointed to earlier studies of this type of basing mode that showed it to be not only more expensive than MPS, but also very unreliable. Congress accepted Tower's assessment of the airmobile mode and rejected it.

In October 1981 the administration decided at last to support the idea of basing the MX in existing Titan and Minuteman silos, which would be "superhardened" to withstand a heavier blast if attacked. Noting the strong support in Congress for the MPS, Weinberger told them that "the Administration intends to explore deceptive basing [MPS] of offensive missiles and defensive components of the BMD program." Meanwhile, Senator William Cohen of Maine echoed widespread Senate sentiment in favor of deceptive basing when he called retrofitting the old silos with new missiles "most ill advised and ill conceived."

With congressional debate centering on a choice between MPS or superhardened silos for nearly a year, the administration surprised everyone when it submitted its long-awaited "permanent" MX basing plan in October 1982. The plan was called closely spaced basing (CSB) but quickly nicknamed Dense Pack. Under CSB all of the MX missiles would be based together in one small field at SAC's 5,872-acre Francis E. Warren AFB near Cheyenne, Wyoming. The rationale for Dense Pack was that with all the missiles so close together, at least some would

survive a direct hit. Nevertheless, survivability under the CSB came into serious question; it was back to the drawing board once again.

By May 1983 the Congress had come back to the idea of basing the MX in Minuteman silos, which it had earlier rejected. The president's Scowcroft Commission had recommended it along with development of a smaller and truly mobile intercontinental missile (SICM). By now, Congress recognized the need for modernizing the ICBM force soon, as well as the need for more bargaining power in arms control talks. Congress approved $625 million for flight-testing and development. On October 14, 1983, the second successful launch of the MX took place from the Pacific Missile Test Center at SAC's Vandenberg AFB on the California coast. The MIRV system was tested with six unarmed reentry vehicles and, as with the earlier flight, the vehicles impacted their target 4,100 nautical miles away in the Pacific, north of the Kwajalein Missile Range. In the first eight MX tests, the missile would be launched from its cannister, then testing would proceed to flights from a modified Minuteman silo located at Vandenberg.

Strategic Planning

Each weapons system in the Triad has its own strengths. The SAC ICBMs have the advantages of immediate readiness, quick reaction time, and the ability to penetrate all known enemy defenses. The Navy's submarine-launched ballistic missiles (SLBMs) have the same readiness and reaction advantages, as well as the protection of mobility. SAC's missiles are in hardened silos impervious to all but direct or near-direct hits, but the Soviets do know exactly where all the silos are located and have almost certainly targeted each of them. The SLBMs, by contrast, are never in the same place, and a moving target is harder to hit than a stationary one; because of their nuclear power plants, the subs can stay submerged at sea for months at a time. Although their mobility makes them harder to hit, it also reduces the SLBM's accuracy, and because the missiles must be enclosed in a submarine, they are a bit smaller and have a shorter range than the land-based ICBMs.

SAC's manned bombers lack the immediate readiness and speed of the missiles but offer a higher degree of flexibility. Bombers can be placed on airborne alert during time of crisis and be recalled to their base when the crisis abates. Missiles cannot be recalled. Once fired, they go all the way. Bombers, once launched, can also be diverted to other targets. Because of their relatively slower speed, bombers are the most susceptible of the legs of the Triad to being intercepted and shot down, although new technology is helping to change that.

To be used effectively, these three separate parts of the Triad must work together: scenarios must be planned, targets selected, and uninterrupted communications assured so that plans and data can be transmitted. The weapons systems are the hardware of the strategic deterrent, but it is the Joint Strategic Target Planning Staff (JSTPS) who writes the program, and the Single Integrated Operational Plan (SIOP) and National Strategic Target List (NSTL) who are the software. The JSTPS was established in August 1960 by the Eisenhower administration Secretary of Defense Thomas S. Gates in reaction to a need to coordinate the strategic nuclear weapons policies of the various services. The JSTPS reports to the Joint Chiefs of Staff (JCS) through its director of Strategic Target Planning (DSTP) who is also the commander in chief of SAC. The JSTPS is composed of a number of SAC personnel who, like their commander, serve a double role, but it also includes representation from the Army, Navy, and Marine Corps. The JSTPS

is in turn divided into two directorates, one of them composed of targeting specialists, whose job it is to continually review the NSTL and the other composed of operations specialists whose job is to come up with the best SIOP to successfully attack and destroy the targets on the NSTL if SAC and/or the Navy are called upon to do so. In addition to representatives from the various U.S. military services on the JSTPS, there are also representatives of various U.S. unified military theater commands—Atlantic, Pacific, and European. To ensure as broad a spectrum as possible, a group of Allied officers from the NATO high command also serves on the JSTPS.

The targets on the NSTL are always classified as secret, though they are not always the same. Originally they included primarily cities and population centers in the USSR, but in recent years the emphasis has shifted to industrial and military targets, including in particular the Soviet ICBM fields.

According to the Carter administration Secretary of Defense, Harold Brown, in his last annual report, there are five classes of targets in the Soviet Union, with cities not specifically included. The primary targets, the nuclear forces, include not only the missile bases (IRBM—intermediate-range ballistic missile—as well as ICBM) but nuclear weapons storage sites, strategic command and control centers, and strategic bomber and submarine bases as well. The secondary targets include other command and control centers, and the tertiary targets include conventional military bases and supply depots as well as military logistics and transportation systems. The fourth and fifth categories include war and other industries, respectively. The former includes munitions and weapons factories, refineries, and rail yards, and the latter, such industries as cement, coal, steel, and electric power.

Although it is no secret that the majority of the targets on this constantly updated list are in the

USSR, targets in other countries are probably added from time to time. For example, it is known that one of the retaliatory options discussed in the wake of the seizure of the U.S. embassy in Tehran in 1979–81 led to contingency plans for nuclear strikes on targets in Iran. It is probably safe to assume that had these strikes taken place they would have been made by aircraft rather than ICBMs.

The SIOP, like the NSTL, is flexible and always changing to take into account such factors as changes in the level of available weapons technology. The SIOP is a final-option type of plan, the kind to be executed only when deterrence and all other methods for preventing attack have failed. It is in itself a major part of deterrence.

The SIOP directorate uses all available intelligence information about Soviet and other nations' intentions and capabilities to create a computer simulation of a variety of potential conflicts. By using a computer model, the directorate can evaluate a variety of scenarios using various combinations of the strategic weapons available in the Triad. War games are played based on real data, and the results help the directorate develop the SIOP, the general war plan for American strategic forces and one of the most comprehensive war plans ever conceived. In preparing the SIOP, the IBM 3033 and IBM 4341 computer systems are used to assign weapons, perform penetration and damage analysis, and determine the timing of aircraft and missile sorties. An IBM 3851 mass storage unit is used to integrate the air-launched cruise missile (ALCM) into SIOP scenarios. All of this data, once formulated, goes to the Mission Data Preparation System (MDPS), where it is used to produce routing tapes for both the ALCM and the bomber carrying it. Meanwhile, the ground-launched cruise missiles are integrated into the SIOP by way of the Theater Mission Planning System (TMPS).

Once completed, the SIOP is documented and analyzed by the Worldwide Military Command and Control System's network of Honeywell 6080 computers. All of the war-gaming is done because, in the event of a real emergency, there would be only six to thirty minutes for the president to order execution of the SIOP; he must have all the options instantly available.

In September 1980 the JSTPS was augmented by another joint agency, the Joint Strategic Connectivity Staff (JSCS). JSCS, like JSTPS, reports to the Joint Chiefs of Staff and has as its director the commander in chief of SAC. The new agency is based at SAC headquarters and has as its responsibility the analysis of the connectivity, or integration, of strategic systems, facilities, and procedures, making recommendations to the JCS concerning the required updating of strategic offensive and defensive operational capabilities. Connectivity is defined as ensuring the compatability and commonality of all the links in the chain of strategic C^3 (command, control, and communications) systems that connect field commanders, commanders in chief, and the national command authorities (the president and the secretary of defense), so that in time of war the SIOP can be quickly and accurately transmitted. The JSCS, composed of about thirty people from the Army, Navy, and Air Force, consults with the commanders in chief responsible for nuclear weapons to ensure the integration of communications both between the commanders and the national command authorities as well as between the commanders and their own commands. Not only do the SAC commander and the president need an immediate, fully comprehensive, and fully up-to-date SIOP, they need a reliable means of transmitting it, because, in time of actual emergency, even the smallest communications malfunction could buy a ticket to disaster.

2 SAC Central

Out in the American heartland, where the great Missouri River carves its way southward and the amber waves of Nebraska grain give way to the cornfields of Iowa, is a modest three-story red brick building nestled quietly in rolling green lawns. Completed in 1957 in bland late-fifties style, it looks like something from a typical midwestern college campus, but nothing could be further from the truth. This building is SAC Central—Building 500, Offutt AFB, Nebraska—the home of a real-life drama more serious than any concocted by the human mind. Below the three visible aboveground stories is a basement, and below that another three-story building. This structure buried under twenty-five feet of earth and reinforced concrete is a carefully crafted self-contained rectangular capsule with more than three acres of floor space. On those three acres are SAC's Command Post, the SAC Automated Command Control System (SACCS), part of the JSTPS, as well as communications, data processing, intelligence, and other support facilities. The walls and ceilings of this underground complex are built of reinforced concrete two feet thick with two ten-inch-thick intermediate floors and a roof that varies in thickness from two to nearly four feet. If SAC were to go to war, the large steel doors of the underground complex would slam shut, and SAC's control center would be sealed off and could operate on its emergency power system, artesian wells, and stored supplies for an extended period.

Above: As spring comes to eastern Nebraska, the trees around SAC Headquarters begin to leaf out. The blue band around the base of the Minuteman monument was common on SAC missiles and bombers until the sixties.

If war were seen to be imminent, the commander in chief of SAC and his staff would make their way to the balcony overlooking the 39-by-149-foot Command Post while members of the battle staff took up stations on the Command Post floor, 46 feet below ground. They all would then be facing six display screens, each 16 feet square, on which the SACCS would use group display generators to project sixteen separate displays simultaneously on the four center screens, while view-graphs were projected on the two side screens. All the information needed by the commander and his battle staff would be immediately available on the screens, including location and status of SAC units, as well as allied and enemy units, and in time of war, the progress of SAC's strike force.

Even in peacetime, the personnel in SAC's Command Post continuously monitor missile warning information, constantly on guard for an ICBM Pearl Harbor. A variety of detection systems, using air- and ground-based sensors as well as satellites, are equipped to detect ICBM or sea-launched ballistic missile attacks against North America or Western Europe as they occur and to transmit that information to the Command Center Processing and Display System terminals at the National Military Command Center under the Pentagon in Washington, the Alternate National Military Command Center at Fort Ritchie in Maryland (which exists as a backup if the Pentagon is destroyed), the North American Aerospace Defense Command (NORAD) headquarters under Cheyenne Mountain in Colorado, and the video display terminals and the huge wall screens of SAC's underground Command Post. The Command Center Processing and Display System, which is managed by the director of Command Control at SAC headquarters, provides threat assessment not only to the JCS, NORAD, and SAC but to the president as well, who is charged with making the decision of whether or not to implement the SIOP.

Doomsday

What would happen if one of those little flecks of green light on the SAC radar scopes really *is* hostile? Someone would touch the president's elbow at a drearily formal state dinner and tell him he had better come take a look. He would excuse himself with a forced smile and hurry from the room, leaving the warm and stuffy world of polite small talk for the cold chill of a deadly game in which his every word and even the spaces between his words may mean life or death for millions.

It's there on the screen. Irrefutable evidence of an incoming Soviet ICBM. Four minutes from launch and hurtling toward Seattle or Albuquerque or even Washington. The president—they call him the National Command Authority—has less than half an hour to act. If he could not have been found, the vice-president would have then become the National Command Authority.

The president picks up the phone and is connected to the Joint Chiefs of Staff by means of the JCS Alerting Network, a secure voice communications system. The SAC commander in turn is always within reach of this Alerting Network, through which he has direct access to the National Military Command Center at the Pentagon as well as to the other commanders. Tonight he happens to be in his office on base clearing up some paperwork, but they could have caught him anywhere. There are telephones in his home and car and in other selected locations in the buildings and offices where he might be found. Once he has been notified, the word goes out simultaneously to the two hundred SAC operating locations around the world by means of SAC's Primary Alerting System (PAS). The PAS, or "Red

Phone" system, is the heart of SAC Command Control Communications, which is managed by the Strategic Communications Division. The PAS is routed to the SAC units through two widely separated Red Phone lines. The primary line goes directly to the bomber wing command posts and to the 152 underground ICBM launch control centers and hardened alternate command posts. The second Red Phone line goes to the same locations by way of the Eighth and Fifteenth Air Force command posts. Ultimately the word will become the "go-code," and will be transmitted to the men in the cockpits and at the missile control consoles. The lights flash and Klaxons sound. Men in OD flight suits dash for the already whining B–52s. Bomber crews in the air await instructions.

In addition to the Red Phone, SAC uses digital transmission media to transmit written communications to the operating locations. These transmissions are by means of the SAC Automated Command Control System (SACCS) and may be transmitted simultaneously to 3000-words-per-minute printers located at all of SAC's North American command posts. Tonight the printers are whirring with unaccustomed fervor. SACCS also manages the computers at SAC headquarters that store and process force status information and project it on the wall screens at SAC headquarters and in the numbered air force command posts, where the big doors have already slammed shut, sealing off these artificial ecosystems for the duration of the present war.

Bathed in the icy glare of the full moon high over the Rockies, a B–52 crew on airborne alert is tied into the network by means of its high frequency (HF), single-sideband radio system, code-named Giant Talk. When the Giant talks, his voice is transmitted via fourteen worldwide ground stations. Because HF radio is not always reliable in the Arctic, where many of SAC's airborne missions are flown, Giant Talk is augmented by Green Pine, a system of ultra high frequency (UHF) radio stations located in an arc stretching across the top of North America from Keflavik, Iceland, to Adak near the tip of the Aleutian island chain. The UHF and HF radio systems are, in turn, backed up by a Survivable Low Frequency Communications System (SLFCS), which operates in the low frequency/very low frequency (LF/VLF) range.

If needed, the Emergency Rocket Communications System (ERCS) will utilize a Minuteman II booster launched from a Minuteman site to place a communications package into a suborbital trajectory. The package would, after separation from the booster, transmit prerecorded information on two UHF frequencies.

Since 1983, an even more sophisticated system has been in use. Tonight, as these critical seconds tick by, much of the communications load is being carried by AFSATCOM, the Air Force Satellite Communications System, of which the SAC portion is code-named Giant Star. AFSATCOM is integrated with the Navy's older Fleet Satellite Communications System (FLTSATCOM) and now provides communications integration to SAC ground and airborne command posts as well as bombers and other aircraft. Giant Star has the potential to render much of the earlier system obsolete, and tonight it is providing a reliable back-up alternative to the ground-based transmitters and relays.

All the communications capability in, or around, the world is, of course, worthless if there is no command post to originate the communications. The SAC Command Post at Offutt is protected from almost anything short of a direct hit by a Soviet warhead. But SAC Central is probably the target of a whole brace of Soviet ICBMs. Armed with this conjecture and the knowledge that in nuclear warfare nothing is invulnerable, SAC de-

Right: The Blackbird in its lair. SR-71 ground crewmen inspect the belly of one of their charges. The business end of the Blackbird, the belly, contains a dazzling variety of cameras and sensors.

Far Right: The flight suit worn by SR-71 crewmen is similar in most respects to the space suit worn by astronauts aboard the space shuttles.

REMOVE BEFORE FLIGHT

veloped an alternative SAC Central, the EC–135 Airborne Command Post, to pick up the baton of command if Offutt were put out of service. Code-named Looking Glass, the EC–135 Airborne Command Post aircraft have been in continuous 24-hour-a-day operation since February 1961. The EC–135 is a Boeing Model 717, very similar to the Boeing Model 707 commercial jetliner and almost identical to the Boeing KC–135 (also Model 717) air-refueling tanker. The EC–135 (*E* for electronics) even has the refueling boom of the KC–135 and can perform aerial refueling. The Looking Glass aircraft are assigned to the 55th Strategic Reconnaissance Wing, the largest operational unit at Offutt, and are operated by two airborne command control squadrons, one at Offutt and one at Ellsworth AFB in South Dakota.

The Looking Glass Airborne Command Post flys a random pattern over the United States, usually on an eight-hour shift, always staying aloft until the next shift's aircraft has taken off and established all necessary communications with SAC headquarters, the National Military Command Center, and the SAC forces on alert around the world. To perform its mission, Looking Glass has aboard the same type of battle staff that are underground at Offutt. The commander, or Airborne Emergency Actions Officer, is a SAC general, and his staff includes experienced command control, operations, plans, intelligence, logistics, and communications personnel. They are equipped with data processing computers and HF, UHF, and LF/VLF communications equipment that allow them to perform the same tasks performed at Offutt and to take control of SAC's strategic nuclear forces and execute the SIOP at the direction of the president or whoever else may be acting as the National Command Authority. The Airborne Launch Control System (ALCS) will also permit Looking Glass to control the entire Minuteman fleet tonight if any or all of the ground launch control centers are put out of action.

While SAC manages its own Airborne Command Post, it also manages that of the Joint Chiefs of Staff and the National Command Authority as well. The National Emergency Airborne Command Post (NEACP, pronounced "kneecap") was introduced in 1974 and is located in a modified Boeing Model 747 jet transport given the Air Force designation E–4. The function of the fleet of four E–4s is to replace the National Military Command Center at the Pentagon if it and the alternate at Fort Ritchie are put out of service or are in danger of being put out of service. In such a case, or in case of general nuclear war, the president, the secretary of defense, and the Joint Chiefs of Staff would all probably operate from the NEACP.

Tonight, twelve minutes after being called away from the table and nine minutes after sending the SAC commander running to the underground command post at Offutt, the president and the secretary of defense (himself a potential National Command Authority) are boarding a helicopter for Andrews AFB, eleven miles away, to board the NEACP. The big white E–4 is waiting at the south end of the Andrews taxiway, a short distance from the passenger terminal and two buildings from the 89th Military Airlift Wing hangar where Air Force One is pampered. Its ominous presence here over the years—waiting fueled and ready for this eventuality—has earned it the nickname "Doomsday Plane." Finally, as the clatter of the incoming Marine helicopter is heard against the whine of the E–4's turbofans, those on hand realize that "doomsday" has finally arrived.

The NEACP is ready for immediate takeoff, and it has first priority for the Andrews runway. Possessing the inherent long range of the 747 and the aerial refueling capabilities of the E–4 derivative, NEACP will be aloft for several days.

Inside, the president and his hastily assembled battle staff settle into their respective work areas in the 4,350 square feet of floor space and go to work. With the communications equipment available to them, they will be able to communicate with American air, sea, and ground forces worldwide. Before the big plane has crossed Chesapeake Bay en route to its station, the president is following up the counterstrike that he ordered earlier from his office. Before the first Soviet ICBM can impact an American target, Minuteman reentry vehicles are plunging back through the atmosphere toward Pinsk and Minsk and Omsk. B–52s high over the Arctic wastelands are releasing cruise missiles bound for the ICBM fields of the Ural foothills and the tank factories of the Ukraine.

This is the doomsday scenario, Mutual Assured Destruction in action. It is the most serious game ever devised, and the fact that SAC is prepared to play it so well has prevented it from being played thus far and will prevent its being played for the indefinite future. As they say in the SAC motto, Peace Is Our Profession.

3 Strategic Reconnaissance

The lifeblood of the Joint Strategic Target Planning Staff, and indeed any strategic planner, is intelligence. To support the needs of the JSTPS and other agencies, SAC operates a fleet of highly secret high-performance reconnaissance aircraft. The reconnaissance data provided by these SAC aircraft is an important part of American strategic planning, verifying Russian compliance with SALT treaties, monitoring military activities of other countries, and providing information for updating the SIOP for nuclear retaliation or other war plans. Recently, satellites have taken a larger role, but aircraft still have many capabilities that cannot be duplicated from outer space.

The aircraft include the Boeing RC–135 (Boeing Model 739), a plane very similar, except for the large radome in its nose, to the Boeing KC–135 Stratotanker and the EC–135 (both Boeing Model 717), the latter being used as the Looking Glass aircraft. The plane itself is quite ordinary (both 717 and 739 airframes are very similar to the familiar commercial 707 jetliner airframe), but the equipment they contain includes some of the most complex radio and radar surveillance sensors yet devised.

From the familiar RC–135, one moves to some of the most unusual aircraft, not only in SAC's inventory, but in any inventory. These include the notorious U–2 and its similar, though considerably modified, offspring the TR–1 and, of course, the highest performance aircraft known to exist anywhere, the SR–71 Blackbird. Beyond their high performance, another unusual characteristic of these aircraft is that they are not based in several squadrons located at various SAC bases around the country as are SAC's bombers, tankers, and even ICBMs. These aircraft are all assigned to a single wing at a single base.

Beale AFB is thirteen miles east of Marysville, California, a couple of hours northeast of San Francisco, where the flat, rich farmlands of California's Central Valley meet the foothills of the Sierra Nevada. There is no small American town more typical than Marysville. It has a small downtown, a main street clogged with high school kids in cars on a Saturday night, a proliferation of fast-food franchises and shopping centers spreading from its edges, quiet tree-lined streets, and tracts of ranch-style housing. The long, straight road leading out to the base (known, appropriately, as Beale Road) is lined with places where you can buy an ice cream cone or a plate of ribs or stop to listen to Hank Williams, Jr., roll out of a jukebox while you shoot pool or drink Lone Star from a long-necked bottle. At the end of the road there is a gate, and that is where the mood begins to change. There is something strange in the air.

Beale AFB was established as the U.S. Army's Camp Beale in 1942 as a training base. The camp was named for Gen. Edward Fitzgerald Beale (1822–1893), one of those characters with which California's early history abounds. A graduate of the Naval Academy, Beale came to California with Commodore Stockton during the Mexican War. He served behind enemy lines with Kit Carson, was in charge of the U.S. Army Camel Corps, and later became Surveyor General of California. Foreclosing on ranchers who were behind with their mortgage payments and buying the ranches for himself at auction, Beale ended up as California's largest landowner.

The foothills of the Sierra begin at the edge of the base. The pastures of the valley yield to tangles of brambles and dry grass that spread up the hillsides of Beale's nearly twenty-three thousand acres, in turn giving way to the pines at the crest of the first hills. High on the hill that dominates the base is the U.S. Air Force Space Command PAVE PAWS early warning radar, which scans the Pacific for evidence of Russian submarine-launched ballistic missiles hurtling toward the nation. As you enter the main gate, the hangars of the spy planes form a low aluminum line stretching across the near horizon about a quarter of a mile ahead. To get there you turn right to come around the south end of the runway. Base housing is located several miles up in the hills, away from the howl of the noisy yet mysterious jets operated by the 9th Strategic Reconnaissance Wing (SRW).

Don't let the word *ninth* be confusing—this is the only wing of its kind in the Air Force. Included within the Wing are the 1st and 99th Strategic Recon Squadrons. The 1st was originally activated in 1913 as the 1st Aero Squadron and has the distinction of being the first squadron in the Air Force. The 99th was activated four years later and, along with the 1st, served in both world wars. The 1st went on to become an observation squadron and later a bomber squadron, becoming a strategic recon squadron at Beale in 1966 as it became the sole operator of the Air Force's fleet of SR–71 Blackbirds. The 99th became a strategic recon squadron with its move to Beale in 1976 and is today the Air Force's worldwide operator of the U–2/TR–1 fleet.

The U–2, like the TR–1 and the SR–71, is a product of Lockheed's "Skunk Works," the highly secret Burbank, California, development center presided over by the great aircraft designer Kelly Johnson. Johnson's designs have often been quite unusual—and frequently very successful. There is no clear definition of his design style. Some of his aircraft, such as the U–2 and the TR–1, have very broad wingspans, whereas others, such as the F–104 and the SR–71, have very short wings. Once, when asked by noted aviation artist Robert Bausch to comment on this, Johnson laughed and said, "It seems like some of my airplanes have too much wing and some don't have enough." In fact, each of his designs, particularly his reconnaissance aircraft, have just the right amount of wing.

Unheralded and unreported, the U–2 rolled from the Skunk Works doors in 1955 in response to an Air Force request for a reconnaissance aircraft that could fly at an altitude in excess of thirteen miles, high above the ceiling of Russian interceptors. The U–2 (*U* for "utility," a designation used to disguise the plane's true purpose) carries electronic sensors as well as radio- and radar-monitoring equipment and cameras. The cameras scan the surface of the earth 70,000 feet below with seven apertures that can cover 275,000 square miles in one mission. Surveillance of Soviet ICBM facilities was of paramount importance, and reconnaissance flights were undertaken over the USSR by U–2s flying between Pakistan and Norway. It was during one of these flights in 1960 that a U–2 piloted by Francis Gary Powers was shot down by a Russian SAM (surface-to-air missile), creating an international incident and catapulting the then still-secret U–2 into international prominence.

The U–2 is basically a turbojet-powered glider, with a long, pencil-like fuselage and broad, straight wings. The glider configuration gives it long endurance and long range. Twenty years after the first U–2As went into service, the basic configuration evolved into the much broader winged U–2R, from which is derived the outwardly identical TR–1 tactical reconnaissance aircraft that first flew in August 1981. The big, black TR–1s, like the U–2R, are 63 feet long with a wingspan of 103 feet, compared with the earlier U–2s, which were 49 feet 7 inches long with an 80-foot span. The TR–1s have a 90,000-foot ceiling compared to 70,000 feet for the earlier U–2s. Although they are based at Beale and remain under SAC control, the TR–1s are rotated through bases in Europe, where they provide tactical reconnaissance support, such as day-and-night all-weather surveillance of potential battle areas, for the United States Air Forces in Europe (USAFE).

Finally, there is the plane that is unlike any other in SAC's inventory or, indeed, any other in the world. The SR–71 Blackbird is undoubtedly one of the great masterpieces of the art of aircraft design. A product of Kelly Johnson's "Skunk Works" in the 1960s, it is the supreme testament to Johnson's extraordinary skill that no aircraft has been created in twenty years to top its performance. This wondrous machine had its genesis in the YF–12 supersonic interceptor program in the early sixties. (One of the YF–12s had been the first aircraft to achieve a sustained speed of Mach 3.) The demonstrated need for that kind of speed was for strategic reconnaissance planes rather than fighters, so the program evolved into the SR–71, with *SR* standing for strategic reconnaissance and the number taken from the Air Force bomber nomenclature since the new aircraft would be assigned to SAC. It is amazing to recollect that the entire development took place without any leaks until President Johnson revealed the plane's existence in 1964.

Serving in Vietnam and over the Middle East during the 1967 and 1973 wars, the SR–71 was an airplane apart, a sinister black bird about which little was known. The speed of the SR–71 was one of the things that set it apart. Up until mid-1964 the world's speed record for the trans-atlantic New York to London route was four hours and forty-six minutes. In September a 9th SRW SR–71 left to cross the Atlantic, arriving at Farnborough near London an incredible *one* hour and fifty-five minutes later. On the return, the Blackbird flew from London to Los Angeles in three hours and forty-seven minutes.

Meanwhile, the Soviet Union had created a high-performance superstar of its own. Designed by the Mikoyan-Gurevich design team, the MiG-25 (NATO code name Foxbat) was developed originally to counter SAC's Mach 2+ B–70 bomber. When the B–70 was scrapped, work continued on the Foxbat, which emerged as the fastest aircraft in the world. Powered by (or, we should say, designed around) two enormously powerful (24,250 pounds of thrust) Tomansky R–31 turbojets, this MiG stunned the West when it was clocked at Mach 3.2 while doing reconnaissance over the Middle East during the 1973 war. In July 1976, in the middle of America's bicentennial year, 9th SRW set out to take the record back from the Foxbat. The SR–71 easily established a new 1000-kilometer closed-circuit speed record of 2092.294 mph and the new world's absolute speed record of 2193.167 mph, records that have yet to be equalled. It is generally accepted that the Blackbirds that took the record were not operating at full power, but just fast enough to take the record. At a 9th SRW briefing it was confidently reported that, if the record should ever be lost, "we'd just take up one of our birds and step down a little harder on the accelerator."

The actual top speed of the SR–71 is a closely guarded secret. The aircrews all wear their patches with the "Mach 3+" insignia and there is a lot of laughter when 4000 mph is mentioned, so it is a good bet that the current world's record is a good deal on the low side for the Blackbird.

It is no small airplane. With a length of 107 feet 5 inches, it is longer than a B–47. When one first sees an SR–71 up close, one is struck by how unlike an airplane it seems. You can't help thinking of it more in terms of a George Lucas fantasy spaceship than a real airplane that is twenty years old. There's something odd about the plane that you can't quite put your finger on until someone points out that "from every angle, it's a different airplane." And it's true. To look at a three-view drawing of the SR–71 is to see three totally different aircraft—one like an arrow, another like a flying saucer, and a third like an enormous bat. Better than 70 percent of the lift is created by the unique contour of the fuselage, with the wings existing as just "something to hang the engines on." The engines, huge Pratt & Whitney JT11D–20B (J58) turbojets, are strange creatures themselves, with massive intake spikes that point down and inward at an acute angle, rather than straight ahead. Airframe distortion at its extreme speed and altitude (the overall length increases by six inches) will be enough to pull the spikes straight when the suction of these intakes produce, by themselves, an incredible 54 percent of the plane's Mach 3 thrust. Another thing you notice about this plane as it is getting ready to launch is that it appears to be sopping wet. To allow for airframe distortion in that strange world inhabited only by airborne Blackbirds the seams of the fuel tanks don't completely seal when the plane is standing still. There is little danger of fire, because of the very high flash point of the J–7 fuel (conventional jets fly on J–4) used only by the SR–71. The J–7 fuel is so nonvolatile that the engines have to be chemically started with polyethyl bromide (PEB). Though called Blackbirds, the SR–71s are officially indigo blue; however, close examination, even in brilliant midday sunlight, reveals a titanium and epoxy surface that could not be a blacker shade of pure, flat black.

Even for the men who fly the Blackbirds, there is a sense of awe. "Faster than a speeding bullet" is a phrase that comes quickly in conversations with SR–71 pilots. Although the SR–71 has the world's absolute altitude record of 85,069 feet and is generally rated with an operational altitude of 80,000, the pilots speak casually of 100,000, and everyone likes to point out that the flight suits these guys wear are of the same design as those worn on the Apollo lunar missions and very similar to the space shuttle suits. Pilots like to tell of flying at extreme altitude, the line that separates day from night clearly visible, and the strange sensation of flying back and forth *between* day and night.

Speed and altitude are the reason for the SR–71, and for all practical purposes, it is impossible to intercept a Blackbird. Though all two dozen SR–71s are based at Beale AFB (except

Above: A Blackbird ready to fly: "This is magic stuff, troops."

for one kept at the Air Force's Plant Two at Palmdale, California), about half of them are on temporary duty around the world, with a permanent detachment based at Kadena AB on Okinawa to keep tabs on North Korea and play cat and mouse with the Foxbats off the Soviet Union's far eastern flank.

The strategic reconnaissance equipment behind the underpanels of the SR–71 is even more highly classified than the plane itself. No public photos of it exist, and only a handful of people have ever seen it. Though pride in their plane runs deep, the pilots also harbor great respect for these wondrous treasures tucked underneath the Blackbird's smooth, thermally emissive skin. "The real beauty," one pilot told this writer, nodding to these unseen machines within the plane's long, smooth belly, "is in what you can't, and will never, see." Among these secrets are surveillance sensors of untold delicacy, and buried behind bottom panels (that for certain missions are replaced with ground glass lenses "heated for fourteen hours to prevent optical distortion") are cameras that can scan 100,000 square miles in an hour, loaded with a special film designed by Kodak that renders minute detail with breathtaking sharpness.

At the leading edge of SAC's arsenal is this airplane so outstanding that its most amazing feats are still classified. It is a miraculous piece of aviation engineering that is, to quote our pilot again, "high-nineties technology that we were lucky to have in the sixties. This is magic stuff, troops, . . . when you strap this mother on . . ."

35

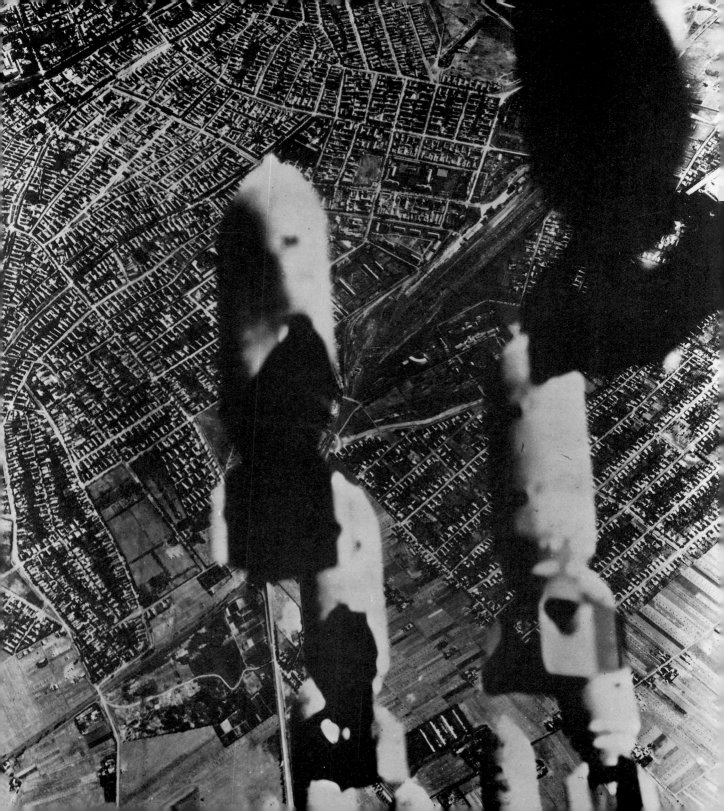

Part II
Strategic Airpower Before SAC

4 Origins of Strategic Airpower

Man first took aircraft into the skies over the battlefields of the First World War simply to observe the enemy, much as he had in balloons during the various conflicts of the late nineteenth century. Aircraft, however, offered the added dimensions of speed and mobility to the warring powers' eyes in the sky. The airborne observer roamed the skies with ease, moving at speeds in excess of a mile a minute. In his bird-like frolic in the heavens, our soaring observer was not alone. Both sides had aeroplanes and aviators, and soon they encountered each other over the trenches. The first encounters were gentlemanly, indeed, probably chivalrous, for our knights of the air had something in common with each other that their respective countrymen on the ground could only dream of.

It didn't take long, I imagine, for the realization to sink in that the enemy with his Mauser trained on your skull saluted the same flag as the silk-scarfed enemy gliding by in his lacquered Sop-

with. Somebody took his sidearm aloft, the first aeroplane went down, and air combat was born. Our aerial warriors soon realized that if they could fly over the enemy's lines to observe, they could fly over the enemy's lines and drop something that exploded. Tactical bombing was born.

Tactical bombing, simply stated, is aerial bombardment of enemy targets, such as troop concentrations, airfields, entrenchments, and the like, as part of an integrated battlefield action at or near the front. Tactical airpower generally is used toward the same goals as, and in direct support of, naval forces or ground troops in the field. Strategic bombing, by contrast, is employed as part of a larger scheme. Strategic targets do not have a direct, traceable connection with what is happening at the front. Strategic airpower is used to strike far behind the lines at the enemy's means of waging war, such as factories, power plants, cities, and ultimately, the enemy's very will to wage war.

Ironically, it was in the same country toward which the Strategic Air Command today casts a watchful eye that the notion of strategic bombing was born. At that time the Russian bear still owed allegiance to the black eagle of the Romanovs. The year was 1913, and the man was Igor Sikorsky, the same man who would amaze the world thirty years later with the first practical hel-

---

Left: USAAF bombs plunge toward a German railhead, 1943.

icopters. The airplane was named Ilya Mouro-metz after the Russian hero of the tenth century, and it was to be the world's first strategic bomber. The big plane was designed as a bomber and powered by four engines, as no other plane before it, with the single exception of its own prototype, the unarmed Russian Knight.

The Ilya Mourometz made its initial flight in May 1913, over a year before the outbreak of the First World War. By December 1914 nearly half of the seventy-five IMs built were already in existence and were formed into the first-ever strategic bomber force. The bomb load of each of the IMs exceeded half a ton, and with a range of nearly four hundred miles, they were able to hit targets well behind the lines in eastern Prussia. The Russians conducted over four hundred raids without the Germans mounting a similar campaign in retaliation, but in the end, other factors intervened. After initial victories, the Russian army was by 1917 defeated on the ground, the Tsar had abdicated and would wind up dead in less than a year, and the events leading to the Russian Revolution were rapidly underway. The Ilya Mourometz had been successful in what it did, but it played only the tiniest part in one of mankind's biggest dramas. Igor Sikorsky emigrated

from Russia to the United States, and the theory of strategic bombing would remain largely dormant in Russia until after the next world war.

Strategic air operations on the western front were soon to follow those in the east. A large squadron of British aircraft attacked German positions in Zeebrugge, Ostend, and other occupied Belgian coastal cities a dozen times between the fifth and twentieth of February, 1915. On March 7, the British flyers bombed a submarine factory in Hoboken, a suburb of occupied Antwerp. The raid was generally successful, with several U-boats reported either sunk or badly damaged.

Shortly after one o'clock on the morning of the twenty-first, the Germans struck back at the Allies, sending a pair of zeppelins over Paris. It was an awesome spectacle, with forewarned French interceptors darting to and fro attacking the huge beasts, awash in the eerie glow of searchlights mounted atop the Eiffel Tower. Huge throngs clogged the streets to watch the action, but after three hours of aerial battle, only about two dozen bombs had been dropped, causing an occasional fire, and the big airships staggered back toward their own lines.

Less than a month later, the German zeppelins were over the eastern coast of England, ranging as far as Newcastle to drop a dozen bombs on a munitions plant there. Raids were also coming perilously close to London, starting fires and, in the words of one contemporary account, "killing two horses." The Bull and George Hotel was reported "completely wrecked" on the night of May 17, and on the night of May 31, after ten months of war, London looked upon its own dead for the first time. Seven were killed, including an elderly "apple woman" who reportedly "died of fright." The first bombs fell on the West End at around eleven thirty, when the lights of the theaters provided a clear target for the attacking zeppelins. The ghostly shapes drifted silently over the Houses of Parliament, picked out by searchlights and picked at by antiaircraft fire. There was panic in the streets. The world was stunned. The largest city in the world, the capital of the British Empire, had fallen victim to aerial bombardment. The next day British bombers made a successful retaliatory raid on a German airship base at Evere, Belgium.

On June 9, Austrian aviators launched the first long-range strategic mission on the southern front, causing several fires in and around St. Mark's Square in Venice. About a week later, the Italians retaliated, hitting the big Austrian naval base at Pola on the Adriatic, where the Austrians based the ships and aircraft they used in attacks on Italian shipping in the northern Adriatic. The following night, June 15, forty-five French bombers attacked Karlsruhe, well beyond the German border, hitting Margrave's Palace and almost killing the German-born queen of Sweden. Though the Germans admitted 19 killed, reliable reports placed the death toll as high as 112, with around three hundred wounded and considerable damage done. It was the most damaging

Above: London searchlights jab the skies above the houses of Parliament during an air raid.

raid to have been made into the German heartland from the west during the war's first year. Warfare had changed: the days when territory beyond the front was immune from attack were forever gone.

Two years later when, after months of immunity to air attack, German Gotha long-range bombers flew unopposed over London, producing several hundred casualties, panic once again ensued. Investigative commissions were appointed. Some British strategic thinkers were farsighted in their appraisal of the situation and insisted that in a future war—indeed, in the present one—strategic air operations could be as significant to the ultimate outcome of the conflict as land and sea operations had been in earlier wars. The relative merits of various theories of strategic bombing were debated in London through the fall of 1917, but it took a renewal of German attacks in the early part of 1918 to finally prompt the British to respond. On April 1 the Royal Air Force was born as a separate service, and plans were laid for a strategic air offensive against the Germany of Kaiser Bill.

British long-range bombers conducted a series of raids on cities in the Ruhr and even ranged

Above: A huge aerial warship over peaceful English fields.

as far south as Frankfurt, but the raids were more strategic bombing experiment than strategic bombing offensive. A full-scale strategic air offensive against Germany was scheduled for the spring of 1919, with Berlin on the target list, but the war ended in November 1918 with the plan untried.

Though the intervention of the United States in the war may have been of pivotal importance to the Allies, American involvement in the air war was not extensive and consisted almost entirely of tactical operations. But strategic air power made an impression on the commander of the American Army Air Service, Col. William "Billy" Mitchell. The commander of the American Expeditionary Force, Gen. John J. "Blackjack" Pershing, saw air power strictly as tactical ground support, the conventional view of the time; Mitchell, however, saw potential for a broader application. He wanted to see the AEF airmen striking the enemy at his source of supply, rather than being simply another weapon for ground commanders. Mitchell became a true exponent of strategic airpower, but his ideas were never implemented. Part of the reason was that strategic bombing, though experimental in Britain and France, was not yet accepted by the American military, whose Army and Navy leaders held very

traditional views. The other part of the reason was purely practical: by the time the Air Service was put into action, the war was almost over.

After the war, there were calls for an American air force, separate and independent from the Army and Navy and with its own strategic direction, like the RAF in Britain. The calls had many voices, but one stood out. Brig. Gen. Billy Mitchell became the central figure in the crusade for independent strategic air power. In effect, he was becoming the godfather of what would one day be the Strategic Air Command.

Mitchell argued that strategic bombers were cheaper to build and operate than battleships, and they could be used faster and more easily to project American power wherever it might be needed around the world. He raised hackles in 1921 when he told Congress that his bombers could sink any ship afloat. To prove him wrong, the Navy agreed to let him try out his theories on some German warships they had inherited at the end of the war that needed to be disposed of. The rules of engagement were written by the Navy's Atlantic Fleet commander. The Navy would regulate the weight of the bombs and the number of planes, and reserved the right to call off the engagement at any time.

On the morning of July 13, 1921, Mitchell and the Army Air Service had their chance against the German ships anchored in the Chesapeake Bay. The first target, a destroyer, went down after forty-four direct hits from 300-pound bombs. The next target was the light cruiser *Frankfurt*. Wave upon wave of planes dropped the specified 300-pounders, but it was still afloat. Mitchell then sent in half a dozen planes with 600-pounders, and they sank the *Frankfurt* in a little over half an hour. Eight days later the heavily armored battleship *Ostfriesland* was the target. This was the ship the Navy hoped would disprove Mitchell's assertions; because of her armor, the ship was considered immune to aerial attack. The attack

Above: The prophet as martyr: General Billy Mitchell *(standing)* during his 1925 trial. He had already proven the value of strategic bombing in modern warfare but his position would not be fully vindicated until World War II, a half-decade after his death.

began with five of Mitchell's bombers lobbing 1000-pound bombs on the *Ostfriesland.* The referees then halted the action to decide if use of new, specially prepared one-ton bombs was to be allowed. They finally relented, and Mitchell ordered in his second wave. A half dozen of the big bombs were dropped in the space of thirteen minutes. Less than ten minutes later, the *Ostfriesland* was on the bottom.

Mitchell had dramatically proven his point and was to do so again and again over the next two years. Everyone seemed convinced of the potential of strategic airpower except the war and navy departments. As Mitchell became more and more outspoken, the Army transferred him from Langley Field in Virginia (too close to Washington for a vocal heretic) to Kelly Field near San Antonio, Texas. In 1925, after the loss of life from the crash of the Navy dirigible *Shenandoah,* Mitchell called the management of national defense by the war and navy departments "incompetent" and "treasonable." The Army had had enough. Mitchell was court-martialed, convicted, reduced to colonel, and drummed out of the service on half pension. He died in 1936, just a few years short of seeing everything he fought for come to pass in World War II. In 1946 Congress voted him a medal "in recognition of his outstanding pioneer service and foresight in the field of American military aviation." The following year he was posthumously granted a major general's commission.

5 Strategic Airpower in Europe

In the 1930s, when Germany set about to rebuild its air force, the major emphasis was on tactical rather than strategic airpower. This is understandable, considering that the commander in chief of the fledgling Luftwaffe was the pompous Hermann Goering, a World War I fighter pilot who had flown with Baron von Richthofen's flying circus and still fancied himself an aerial knight. The design of the Luftwaffe was basically twofold. First came air superiority, the doctrine of controlling the skies over any battlefield. For this purpose, the Luftwaffe developed fast and maneuverable fighters, notably, the outstanding Messerschmitt Bf–109. Second came classical tactical airpower, with medium bombers to strike staging areas behind the lines in advance of ground forces, and light bombers or attack planes, notably, the dreaded Junkers Ju–87 Stuka dive bomber, to operate in conjunction with ground forces.

Because of the tactical air bias of its leadership, the Luftwaffe had not seriously integrated long-range strategic air operations into the overall blueprint. The German armed forces were designed around Hitler's plan to achieve domination of Europe by intimidation through threatened use of the well-oiled war machine or, failing this, lightning fast thrusts at the enemy's jugular. There was seen to be no need for long-range airpower to gradually wear down an adversary. The German successes had supported this belief.

Then came the Battle of Britain. The most powerful army and air force the world had yet seen sat at the south side of the Channel. Hitler assumed that the English would surrender or at least be willing to dicker for a cease-fire. They didn't and they weren't, and Hitler was confused and enraged. He called in his advisors; among them was Hermann Goering, who suggested that his Luftwaffe could defeat Britain from the air and pave the way for the invasion. On paper it looked good for Goering. He had over eight hundred medium bombers, nearly three hundred Stukas, and almost a thousand fighters at scores of bases less than a hundred miles from the coast of England; the Royal Air Force had barely six hundred first-line fighters to hold them off.

For the first time the Germans faced an obstacle they could not readily surmount with blitzkrieg tactics. Though the German army and air force were all-powerful, their navy was not. They lacked the landing barges to cross the Channel and they lacked the surface fleet to cover a cross-Channel invasion. For the first time, the German legions needed time, and Goering's Luftwaffe would buy it.

The Battle of Britain, the first strategic air offensive in history, began on Adlertag ("the Day of the Eagle"), August 13, 1940. Goering's airmen flew nearly fifteen hundred sorties to England on Adlertag and nearly eighteen hundred two days later. It was to be a grueling month, with both sides taking heavy losses. The Germans were beginning to realize that their failure to develop a long-range, four-engine strategic bomber (as the British and Americans had) might cost them the battle. The Heinkel He 111 and Dornier Do 17 medium bombers could reach the London area but lacked the range to successfully carry out operations in the industrial Midlands. Furthermore, the German fighter planes escorting the bombers, the ones that had achieved supremacy in the skies over Europe, did not have the range to carry out sustained combat over England. Frequently they would have to break off in the middle of a dogfight and dash back to refuel in France.

The only combat aircraft in the Luftwaffe arsenal that came close to filling the long-range strategic bomber role was Focke-Wulf's Fw 200. Originally a prewar Luft-Hansa airliner, the big four-engined plane had flown nonstop on the Berlin to New York passenger run, thus it had the required range. But range was about all it had. It was to prove entirely inadequate as a strategic bomber, lacking the power, bomb capacity, armor, defensive armament, and most of all, structural integrity required. The Fw 200 never saw sustained service in strategic operations and was used almost entirely to attack Allied shipping in the North Atlantic beyond the range of fighter protection.

Despite losses and the shortcomings that limited its scope of activity, the Luftwaffe bomber force was doing a terrifyingly good job of completing its assigned task. About ten days into the Battle of Britain, the Luftwaffe high command realized that their primary obstacle was the RAF Fighter Command. Therefore, they decided to concentrate on the Fighter Command's bases, operations centers, and radar net. This decision could have been the turning point of the war, for after less than two weeks of relentless attacks, the Fighter Command was on the verge of collapse. Not only were massive numbers of irreplaceable pilots and aircraft lost, but airfields were being put out of action for days at a time, rendering inoperable planes that hadn't been damaged. Beyond this, the loss of radar and communications severely hampered the aircraft that were still flying. Had the Luftwaffe continued attacks at that level for a week to ten days longer, the RAF would have been defeated, and nothing would have stood in the way of Operation Sea Lion, the invasion of Great Britain.

But fate intervened. Throughout the Battle of Britain the British had attempted to jam or distort the radio beacons on which the German bombers relied for navigation during nighttime raids.

Above: As a pre-war airliner, the Fw 200 proved that it could reach New York, but as a wartime bomber it only proved to be a disappointment.

During the first week of September, a Heinkel on a routine mission, its navigation jammed, got off course and couldn't find its assigned target. Spotting some lights below, the Germans unknowingly unloaded their bombs on downtown London. The British government was enraged and ordered the RAF Bomber Command to bomb Berlin in retaliation. Hitler and Goering had promised the German people that Berlin would never be bombed, so when the raid came on the sixth of September the führer was hysterical. Despite protests from his field commanders, Goering ordered that the offensive against the Fighter Command bases, so near to success, be abandoned in favor of attacks on London and other principal English cities. The Fighter Command was given a break and would be allowed to rebuild. Though the battle was not over yet, this was the turning point, the point after which the German strategic air offensive was doomed to failure.

The "Blitz" on London was far more visible and the loss of life more devastating than in the early part of the battle, but its strategic effect was to strengthen the resolve of the British people to hold out against the Germans. Throughout September German formations of up to a thousand planes appeared over London and the cities of southeast England. The Fighter Command, its bases off the target list and its numbers replenished from factories out of range of the German medium bombers, rose to meet the Luftwaffe assault. By mid-October the tide had finally turned. On the twelfth, Hitler canceled Sea Lion.

The Blitz continued, though; there were constant raids on London, and the center of Coventry was completely destroyed on the nights of October 14 and 15. Despite the relentless raiding, antiaircraft defenses continued to improve, and the bombers paid an ever-higher price for the damage they inflicted. By May 1941, with the level of British raids against German targets surpassing the level of the now-sporadic German raids on England, history's first strategic bomber offensive had ended in failure. Over forty thousand civilians were killed in the eight months of the Battle of Britain, with the Germans losing nearly eighteen hundred aircraft to nearly a thousand lost by the RAF.

In 1944 Germany resumed the air assault on the British Isles, but the overall picture had changed dramatically since 1940. The United States and the Soviet Union were in the war, and the Russians had the Germans on the defensive across a thousand-mile front. A German strategic air offensive against Russia had, despite sporadic raids on Moscow, failed to materialize. Russia's vast area was quite simply too much for the range of medium bombers. In the first years of the war with Russia, the Germans successfully used their blitzkrieg to swiftly advance for hundreds of miles and capture strategic targets. However, though the Germans could capture *hundreds* of miles, the Russians, unlike the Poles or the French, could fall back into *thousands* of miles of territory. Eventually the Germans fell victim to the Russian winters, the vast manpower of the Red Army, long supply lines stretched thin and breaking, and finally, of course, their inability to bomb the Russian in-dustrial plant, which had been moved out of their reach in and beyond the Urals.

The Russians had no strategic air arm either, so the war on the eastern front consisted of two great armies, supported by tactical airpower, locked in the greatest land war in history.

When Germany resumed the Battle of Britain in 1944, the weapons employed were weapons that would have been the stuff of science fiction in 1940. The technological advances made during World War II were unlike those of any other period in this century, and the Germans, overall, were the undisputed leaders. Had the weapons of 1944 been in their arsenal of 1940, the Thousand Year Reich would have lasted longer than its eventual twelve.

Experiments with rockets had been going on for years in several countries, but in Germany, under such scientists as the brilliant Dr. Werner von Braun, rocket research was further advanced. In 1937 the Peenemünde Research Station on the Baltic coast was established, and work began on a series of rockets that would lead up to the awesome A–4. The A–4 would carry a ton of high explosives for at least one hundred fifty miles at speeds so great nothing could come close to catching or stopping it. It was, to use today's parlance, an intermediate-range ballistic missile (IRBM). In the early years of the war, such far-out weapons were not given funding priority largely because Hitler and the high command didn't think the war would last more than eighteen months; anything that would take longer than that to develop was considered superfluous. In October 1942 the A–4 was the subject of a successful test-firing, but it languished in its experimental status for over a year because of disinterest in high places and because of an auspicious British air raid on Peenemünde in 1943.

Meanwhile, another weapon was being developed. It was the pulse-jet-powered Fieseler Fi

Above: One of Germany's few attempts at a strategic bomber, the Me 264 Amerika-Bomber was designed to bomb America but never flew the mission.

103 (or FZG–76), but better known by the name the führer himself gave it: Vergeltungswaffe 1 ("Vengeance Weapon 1") or simply V–1. The V–1 was, to again use today's parlance, a ground-launched cruise missile. Launch sites were built across northern France throughout late 1943. By this time, the Luftwaffe no longer controlled the skies over Europe, so Allied aircraft were able to identify and destroy many of the sites. The V–1s were finally put into service, but not until a week after the Allied invasion of France in June 1944. The second Battle of Britain had begun, but this time it was clearly too little too late. Even though pulse-jet-powered, the speed of the V–1 was just roughly that of the fastest Allied interceptors. Because it had no maneuverability, if the V–1 could be spotted, it could usually be shot down.

By this time, though, the A–4 was ready. Hitler had seen it test-fired. He crowed with delight over a weapon he had once given lowest priority. The A–4 became his Vengeance Weapon 2. The first A–4, or V–2, was launched against England on September 8, 1944. The Germans at last had the ultimate strategic weapon. Had it been given top priority earlier, it could have changed the course of the war. Because the V–2 traveled faster than the speed of sound, it could

not be heard, and no interceptor could catch it. It arrived without warning and created horrible carnage and devastation wherever it landed. Over a thousand V–2s were used against England (between September 8, 1944, and March 27, 1945), and over thirteen hundred were used against Antwerp, Belgium, which by autumn 1944 was the major port supplying the Allied armies in Europe. In addition, just over one hundred fifty were used on Brussels and Liège after they fell to the Allies; fifteen were launched against Paris; and nearly a dozen were used in an attempt to destroy the Rhine bridge at Remagen that the Allies had captured intact in their final push into the Reich in the spring of 1945.

The V–2 was just one more prime example of the great strides made by German technology during the war, another "secret weapon" whose true strategic potential was not recognized until it was too late. In the end, the missile and its creator, Dr. von Braun, fell into the hands of the Americans and were transported to White Sands, New Mexico, where the Peenemünde research continued, ultimately producing the missiles that now fill the inventory of the Strategic Air Command.

Although the German lack of foresight about the need for strategic airpower early in the war prevented them from ever mounting an attack against the United States, it is worth pointing out that by 1944 this was the subject of serious consideration. There were no true strategic bombers in the Luftwaffe inventory at the beginning of the war, but there were several on the drawing boards. The Messerschmitt Me 264 studied in 1941 and designated Amerika-Bomber, first flew in late 1942. It was a four-engine bomber with a range of over nine thousand miles and a 45-hour endurance. The plane wasn't given priority until after the Allied invasion of Europe in 1944; at that time it was the object of power plant experiments that found it alternatively retrofit-

Above: The RAF Bomber Command's Lancasters were among the best strategic bombers of World War II.

ted with turboprop engines and turbojet engines. Ultimately, the Me 264 project was a victim of the Allied strategic air offensive and never found itself over the Atlantic setting a course for New York or Boston.

The German scientists were also at work on another rocket, this one earmarked for the United States. Designated A–9/A–10, the weapon was the world's first two-stage rocket. With a range of over three thousand miles, it was also the world's first intercontinental ballistic missile (ICBM). The rocket consisted of the massive A–10, four times the size of the A–4, as the first stage and either the A–4 or A–9 rocket as the second stage, which would continue the flight as the A–10 cut out and dropped off. Beginning its flight at an altitude of thirty-five miles, the A–9 would have a velocity of around 6000 mph, allowing it to cover twenty-five hundred miles in

about half an hour. As it turned out, no A–10 ever was launched from Peenemünde and no A–9 ever fell on Philadelphia. It is the object of conjecture whether or not by late 1944 or early 1945 such an attack would have affected the outcome of the war. Such conjecture is further qualified, though, by the fact that the Germans were working, ultimately unsuccessfully, on the same kind of secret nuclear weapon that the United States was to explode in the New Mexico desert in the summer of 1945.

Britain's strategic bombing offensive against the German Reich began in 1940 with sporadic bombing during daylight hours. The Royal Air Force decided after the first few months of the war that daylight bombing was too costly in terms of aircraft losses, and that night bombing, though less precise, could be accurate enough in attacks on specific targets. The specific targets selected were refineries and factories, with marshaling yards designated as secondary targets. The large number of attacks on secondaries such as the yards at Hamm are indicative of the difficulty the RAF had in finding specific primary targets by night. In May and June 1941 the RAF made a concentrated effort against the marshaling yards in the Ruhr, figuring that targets so vast would ensure success. The offensive was a failure, so the whole notion of precision bombing was abandoned in favor of the new concept of area bombing.

The area bombing strategy was intended to fill in until precision bombing could be perfected and reinstituted. Early in 1942, however, Arthur "Bomber" Harris became chief of the RAF Bomber Command. Harris felt that area bombing held the key to a successful overall strategy. Noting the efficiency with which the Germans were rebuilding the destroyed targets, Harris asserted that the German will to wage war could only be successfully destroyed by attacking their cities. The area bombing campaign began in the summer of 1942 with the first thousand-plane raids on Essen and Köln. Because Hitler had said that Berlin would never be bombed, it was probably somewhat disconcerting when British bombers began showing up overhead every other night or so.

During the first period of the strategic air offensive against Germany, bomb tonnage increased eightfold, from 31 tons to 2,451 tons between the first and second quarters of 1940. In 1941 the tonnage steadily increased, and by midyear averaged 12,000 tons. This dropped to about half over the winter, but with Harris at the helm of Bomber Command and the Americans in the war, tonnage averaged about 14,500 for the last three quarters of 1942.

The second period in what was now a combined bomber offensive began with the Casablanca Conference of Allied leaders in January 1943. Out of the conference came the first joint plans of operations for the overall combined Allied offensive against Fortress Europe. The objective of the strategic air forces was "the progressive destruction and dislocation of the German military, industrial, and economic system, and the undermining of the morale of the German people to a point where their capacity for armed resistance is fatally weakened."

The primary targets were, in order of priority: (1) U-boat factories and pens, (2) the German aircraft industry, (3) transportation facilities, and (4) the German petroleum industry. A footnote attached to the directive indicated that the "order of priority may be varied from time to time according to developments in the strategic situation. Other objectives of great importance either from the political or economic point of view must be attacked." The object was to give the air force field commanders maximum flexibility in dealing with situations as they arose in the field, a flexibility that SAC commanders were not to enjoy in two subsequent wars.

The RAF continued its nightly area bombing while the U.S. Eighth Air Force in England and Fifteenth Air Force in southern Europe assumed the task of daylight precision raids. By May 1943 it became clear that detection and destruction of U-boats at sea was more effective, and the U-boat pens ceased to be a priority target. In June a new directive came down from the Combined Chiefs of Staff that placed the German aircraft industry at the head of the target priority list. Despite the rapidly growing bomber strength of the Allied air forces, the German fighter strength was rapidly increasing, and the Allies had failed to achieve the air superiority that was necessary before any attempt could be made to invade the heavily fortified northern tier of Europe. In June

of 1943 German aircraft production stood at about twenty-five hundred units per month compared to a monthly average of nine hundred in 1941 and about twelve hundred in 1942. The trend would clearly have to be reversed.

The offensive got off to a slow start in the second half of 1943 with only seven major raids against aircraft production centers. This was because these centers were located or relocated in southern Germany, Austria, and Czechoslovakia beyond easy range of Allied bombers and would have to wait for the more advanced B–17G and B–24J aircraft that were beginning to come on line. Setting these plums aside momentarily, Allied commanders decided to go after a more attainable target. The target chosen for attack was the ball-bearing industry, selected because it was essential to all other industries and because it was concentrated in only three cities. The glittering prize of half the industry's total capacity was located at Schweinfurt. The Eighth Air Force hit Schweinfurt on August 17 and again on October 10, inflicting serious and lasting damage. The bombers, however, were unescorted because the target was beyond range of Allied fighters, and they took a severe mauling from Luftwaffe air defenses, losing nearly 30 percent. Hence the Allied air command was back again to the need to cut into German fighter strength.

For the second period of the air offensive against the Reich, comprising the year of 1943, bomb tonnage was greatly increased, up a quarterly average of 50,000 tons, as against 13,000 tons for 1942, reaching a peak of 66,159 tons in the third quarter.

The third period of the strategic air offensive comprised the period from the beginning of 1944 through the invasion of Europe in June. By now

---

Left: Spilling contrails in their wake, USAAF B-17Gs drive at high altitude toward the heart of the German Reich.

the Allied strategic air forces not only had the best long-range bombers (except the B–29, which was earmarked for the air offensive against Japan) but had long-range fighter protection for the bombers in the form of the P–51D. Both the RAF Bomber Command and the U.S. Eighth Air Force could field in excess of a thousand heavy bombers, while the U.S. Fifteenth Air Force had nearly six hundred. Weather was not cooperative, and the offensive didn't get under way until the last week of February, when 4000 tons of bombs were unloaded on the German aviation industry. The raids continued, with the Germans dealt a reeling blow. Though aircraft production continued to increase (thanks to Albert Speer's masterful management of the German war economy) to a monthly average of over four thousand units between July and September 1944, the offensive put it into a permanent and precipitous decline. It was off by over 25 percent by January 1945. The first two quarters of 1944 saw the 50,000-ton quarterly bomb tonnage of 1943 more than double twice, to 114,360 and 333,556.

The fourth and final period of the strategic air offensive comprised the latter half of 1944 and the first four months of 1945, ending with the defeat of the Reich. The period began with British and Americans having a land presence on the continent and Russians on the verge of capturing the oil fields of Rumania and the vast refinery center at Ploesti that provided the Germans with their sole source of nonsynthetic oil. The decision was made, therefore, to make the denial of synthetic oil to the Germans the primary aim of the strategic air forces. During this period, with both the USAAF and RAF flying precision bombing missions around the clock, 555 separate attacks were made against 135 different targets, including synthetic oil plants, refineries, oil storage facilities, and in general every major target. At the same time, the strategic air forces directed a secondary campaign against

49

50

tank and motor vehicle factories. Between November and February rail transportation facilities assumed the second priority. By March 24 the Ruhr was successfully cut off from the rest of Germany, Allied troops had crossed the Rhine, and most of the German national rail system was either destroyed or paralyzed. During this final period, over a million tons of bombs were dropped.

The incredible increase in bomb tonnage dropped in the war's last ten months delivered a painful and probably decisive blow to the German war economy. Prior to mid-1943, with about 10 percent of the total tonnage having been expended, the offensive had made no serious dent in German armament production or in the overall gross national product, although the area bombing by the British did considerable localized damage that required diversion of labor and resources for repair and cleanup. In the latter half of 1943, a 13 percent loss in tank and motor vehicle production and a 5 percent loss in overall armament production was effected. During the first half of 1944, with the USAAF now present in strength, repeated raids were possible deep into the Reich. Overall production was off by something like 15–20 percent, with ball bearings down an estimated 66 percent. Fighter plane production capacity was 70 percent destroyed in February–March but quickly rebounded and, as we have seen, continued to increase until midyear. Air raid casualties were not as numerous as one might suppose, accounting for less than one percent of the labor force. Nearly 20 percent of the nonagricultural labor force, however, was diverted from other production by chores created as a result of the raids, such as cleanup,

Above: A USAAF B-17G drops a string of 500 pounders on *Festung Europa.*

reconstruction, and dispersal of factories to less vulnerable sites. As to the effects of bomb damage on the civilian economy, the U.S. Strategic Bombing Survey concluded that there was no evidence that shortages of civilian goods ever reached a point at which the German authorities were forced to divert resources from war production in order to prevent disintegration on the home front. What can be said is that the bombing destroyed a substantial part of the consumer goods cushion, thereby preventing any further conversion of civilian goods production to war production in 1944.

After December of 1944 the situation in Germany deteriorated rapidly. Final output decreased drastically across the board because stockpiles of subassemblies that could no longer be produced ran out. Raw material production, which had been in a critical situation for six to twelve months, collapsed. In mid-February 1945

Left: The August 1943 low level raid by USAAF B-24s on Ploesti, Rumania, was a major strategic bombing effort and a first step in knocking out Germany's primary oil refining center. Though it took several raids to knock it out, loss of Ploesti finally forced the Germans to rely on synthethic fuels.

coal deliveries were at 25 percent of normal. Two weeks later they were at 16 percent, and by the end of March they were at 4 percent. Albert Speer, who was the minister in charge of the German economy, wrote in his report of March 15 that the economy "is heading for inevitable collapse within four to eight weeks." On May 7 the Germans signed the unconditional surrender. The U.S. Strategic Bombing Survey concluded that "even if the final victories that carried the Allied armies across the Rhine and Oder had not taken place, armament production would have come to a virtual standstill by May. The German forces, completely bereft of ammunition or motive power, would almost certainly have had to cease fighting by June or July 1945. In the actual case, the collapse occurred before the time when the lack of means would have rendered further resistance impossible."

6 Strategic Air Offensive in the Pacific

At a little past seven on a Sunday morning in December 1941, the pleasant morning calm over Honolulu was broken by the sound of aircraft—many aircraft—then gunfire, then explosions. Swarms of Japanese fighters and attack planes from six aircraft carriers 275 miles north of Hawaii were attacking the invincible battleships of America's Pacific Fleet on "Battleship Row" at the big U.S. naval base in Pearl Harbor. The attack came without warning and lasted less than two hours. When the last raider flew off over the hills, the battleships *Arizona* and *Oklahoma, California* and *West Virginia* had been sunk and four other battleships severely damaged. In addition several hundred aircraft had been destroyed, and over four thousand Amer-

icans had been killed or wounded. It was the most famous air attack of the war and perhaps the most important defeat in United States military history. The ghostly hand of Billy Mitchell had returned from the grave to lie gently on the shoulders of those who had court-martialed him as if to say, "I told you so."

Throughout the late 1930s relations between the United States and Japan deteriorated while Japan's cooperation with Nazi Germany increased. The Japanese-American Treaty of Commerce had been allowed to expire, and the United States insisted on a Japanese withdrawal from China before relations could be normalized. The talks between the two nations were at an impasse. Japan feared that the United States was presenting a serious obstacle to the Greater East Asia Co-Prosperity Sphere—an obstacle that would have to be eliminated.

The principal way that the United States projected its presence in the Far East was by means of its Pacific Fleet. Therefore, it was determined that a pre-emptive strike to cripple the U.S. Pacific Fleet would put the United States out of action long enough for the empire to establish control over Southeast Asia. Japan already had tacit permission from Hitler to occupy the colonies whose mother countries the Nazis had conquered, such as French Indochina and the Netherlands East Indies. To this they would add Burma, Malaya, and the Philippines, America's largest colony. With the Greater East Asia Co-Prosperity Sphere a *fait accompli,* the Japanese would be able to negotiate some sort of treaty or settlement with the United States.

Their pre-emptive strike was a huge success for the Japanese. They had used airpower against a major naval force and had scored a huge victory. Anyone who had still doubted Billy Mitchell's foresight the day before had been converted. As the victorious samurai celebrated aboard their carriers and the United States picked through the debris of the humiliating surprise attack, there were few on either side who doubted the potential of strategic air power.

There were to be no more air attacks against U.S. territory, though they would continue to be dreaded and predicted for close to three more years. In a little over four months, though, American planes would appear in the skies over Tokyo.

After Pearl Harbor and the desperate losing battle in the Philippines, American morale was in need of a lift. Beyond the morale factor, the strategic situation demanded that some action be taken to demonstrate to Japan the serious resolve with which the United States intended to pursue the war. The plan that evolved was similar to the plan of attack that the Japanese had used. Although neither side had strategic bombers of sufficient range to hit each other, they both had aircraft carriers. Japan had used carriers to extend the range of its aircraft, and the United States would do so as well. Specially modified USAAF B-25 medium bombers would be carried within six hundred miles of Japan itself. Turnabout was fair play.

The bombers, under the command of Lt. Col. Jimmy Doolittle, lumbered off the deck of the USS *Hornet* in the early morning of April 17, 1942, bound for Tokyo, Yokohama, and several other Japanese cities. The Doolittle raid caused little bomb damage to the targets—but it was a psychological blow to Japanese home front morale and to the Japanese perception of their own vulnerability. The Japanese had destroyed most of Pearl Harbor, but the Americans had bombed the Japanese capital, a feat that the knights of the Rising Sun could not equal. Despite the strategic value of the raid, the USAAF knew it could not be repeated. All the planes and many of the pilots were lost in forced landings in China; it was simply too costly. What was needed was a bomber with the range to contend with the vast distances of the Pacific. Such a plane was on the drawing boards and was soon to become a top secret, top priority reality. The plane was Boeing's B-29 Superfortress, and it was to be the single most important element in USAAF's strategic air offensive against Japan.

By 1944 the B-29 was ready to go to war. Bases had been prepared for it in and around Ch'eng-tu, China, with the Twentieth U.S. Army Air Force (composed of the 20th and 21st Bomber Commands) created as the B-29 operating unit. The Superfortresses began to arrive on station in April and flew their first mission, against Japanese-held Bangkok, Thailand, on June 5. Ten days later sixty-eight B-29s flew the first mission against Japan proper since the Doolittle raid more than two years earlier. The target was Yawata, and the results were disappointing. The B-29s and the 20th Bomber Command were having teething trouble. Army Air Force commander Henry H. "Hap" Arnold brought Brig. Gen. Curtis LeMay in to reorganize the show. LeMay revamped procedures, and efficiency improved.

By the fall of 1944 Guam and the Mariana Islands in the mid-Pacific had been recaptured from the Japanese. Air bases that would be home to the 21st Bomber Command and the staging area for the final strategic air offensive against Japan were under construction on Guam, Saipan, and Tinian. These bases would put the B-29s much closer to their targets. On November 24, the "Superforts" flew their first mission from the Marianas, against the Nakajima aircraft works just outside Tokyo. The raid was a success insofar as the B-29s located and bombed a target in the heart of Japan with the loss of only one of their number, but subsequent raids suffered teething trouble similar to what the 20th Bomber Command had experienced when they began operating from China. The strategic air offensive was one of General Arnold's pet projects, so he decided to move Curtis LeMay, who had shaped up the 20th in China, to the Marianas to work with the 21st. LeMay arrived in the Marianas in late January 1945.

After a month of careful observation, LeMay issued the orders that changed the whole ball game for the 21st. The new primary targets would be (in a reflection of what had come earlier in Europe) aircraft engine plants, followed by airframe factories and the cities that surrounded both, which meant just about every major city in Japan but Kyoto. LeMay then went on to completely reverse just about everything else about the way the 21st did business. Precision high-altitude bombing would give way to area bombing from lower altitudes. Day bombing would give way to night bombing, and incendiaries would replace high explosives. Area bombing would compensate for the difficulty encountered in locating precise targets under heavy cloud cover, and incendiaries dropped by the lead B–29s would set fires that would guide other planes to the target. The change of tactics would catch the Japanese off guard, and they had no significant night-fighter force with which to counteract it.

LeMay's first raid employing the new *modus operandi* was scheduled for the night of March 9/10, 1945, with the heart of Japan's capital city designated as primary, secondary, and tertiary target. Over three hundred B–29s carrying napalm and clusters of incendiaries lifted off from the Marianas on the afternoon of the ninth and arrived over Tokyo after dark. The raiders dropped their firebombs all across the city, creating hundreds of fires in the wood and paper houses that rapidly spread into a single gigantic, roaring inferno. Updrafts sucked huge pillars of flame into the air, creating a fire storm of monstrous proportions. The raid was to be recorded as the most fearsome of the entire war, surpassing in destruction even the nuclear attacks that were to follow. Sixteen square miles of Tokyo became a smoldering charcoal desert, de-

void of any recognizable fragment of what had been there before. Over a hundred thousand people were killed or wounded, and a million survivors had no housing. Fourteen B–29s were lost to enemy action. Japan's attack on Pearl Harbor had been remembered and avenged.

In the next week the whole process was repeated in Osaka, Kobe, and twice at Nagoya. With the major centers of the home islands smoldering, the B–29s in April switched to tactical raids on Okinawa to soften it up for the impending invasion. In May, their incendiary stocks replenished, the 21st Bomber Command once again resumed the firebombing of Japan's major cities and the mining of Japanese coastal waterways. Japan's ability to wage war was being seriously eroded, as was the home-front morale.

Between June 1944 and February 1945, the Twentieth Air Force had dropped just over 10,000 tons of bombs on Japan, with the December to February average standing at around 2000. In March and April, with LeMay now in charge, the monthly average increased to over 15,000. By June the tonnage had more than doubled, and in July it was well over 42,000 tons. Half that amount was dropped in the first half of August prior to the capitulation of Japan.

With Germany defeated, the Allies began to plan for the final assault on the Japanese home islands. To augment the roughly one thousand B–29s that LeMay had available in the Marianas and the several thousand more B–29s that would be produced by the end of 1945, thousands of USAAF and RAF planes in Europe could now be diverted to the fray. These planes could be based on newly won islands, such as Iwo Jima, much closer to Japan than the Marianas.

Nevertheless, the task ahead was sobering. Looming on the horizon for Allied leaders was the prospect of having to invade the Japanese home islands. Given their fierce and fanatical defense of smaller islands like Iwo Jima and

Above: A group of 29th Air Force B-29s during a 1944 raid.

Okinawa, the Japanese would no doubt put up the bloodiest battle ever encountered. Despite destruction of the cities, the Japanese army was still strong and bent on a suicidal defense of the homeland. Operation Olympic would be the first thrust in the operation. Coming in November 1945, it was designed to secure the southern island of Kyushu in advance of the invasion of the main island of Honshu, Operation Coronet, which would come with a mass landing south of Tokyo in March 1946. The overall operation could last well into 1947 and could cost two million Allied casualties.

While the final invasion was being planned in high places, another option was under consideration in higher places. Meanwhile, in June 1945, a special unit within the Twentieth Air Force 21st Bomber Command was forming on Tinian. The 509th Composite Wing (which was to play an important role in the early years of the Strategic Air Command) was designed for a single type of mission, with a secret, as yet untested, weapon. The overall strategic purpose of the 509th—its mission and its secret weapon—was to eliminate the need to invade Japan and thus save two million Allied lives.

The planes were specially modified B-29s, the weapon was the atomic bomb, and the first mission was flown on August 6, 1945, with Hiroshima as the primary target, Kokura, the secondary. At a quarter past eight one bomb fell on Hiroshima and seventy-eight thousand people perished instantly in a fireball brighter than a thousand suns. The Japanese warlords were unsure what had happened and were at a loss for what to do. Three days later, the 509th flew again, this time with Kokura, the primary target, obscured by clouds. Shortly before noon, the secondary target, Nagasaki, disappeared under a mushroom cloud. Less than a week later the Japanese Empire agreed to unconditional surrender; World War II was over.

Part III
SAC's Formative Years

7 The Creation of SAC

During the course of World War II, the USAAF had grown from a prewar strength of 23,455 personnel, by a *thousand* percent, to 2,373,292. It was the largest air force in terms of both personnel and planes that the world had ever seen and nearly four times the size of the largest air force of today.

In the euphoria that followed the signing of the official surrender documents in Tokyo Bay in September 1945, the United States began swiftly demobilizing its forces, discharging its uniformed manpower, and deactivating vast portions of the command structure. Tens of thousands of aircraft were sold for scrap. The B–17 and B–24 fleets that once numbered nearly thirty thousand were virtually eliminated. The number of B–29s, the largest and most sophisticated strategic bomber to come out of the war, fell from over two thousand to less than two hundred. Of the three numbered air forces that had constituted the strategic air arm of the USAAF, the Fifteenth had been deactivated and the Eighth and the Twentieth, greatly reduced in strength, were now based in the western Pacific.

On March 21, 1946, a first step was taken to-

Left: The Skybolt missile, a forerunner of today's ALCMs, was intended to be deployed aboard SAC B-52s and RAF Vulcans, but the program was scrapped amid controversy in 1962.

ward the long-awaited establishment of a separate and independent U.S. Air Force. The role of the new USAF would be to organize and equip air forces, develop weapons and tactics, provide for air defense, and prepare for strategic air operations in the event of war. The Continental Air Forces of the USAAF were divided into three separate components—the Tactical Air Command, the Air Defense Command, and the Strategic Air Command. SAC's first headquarters was the former Continental Air Forces headquarters at Bolling Field (later Bolling AFB) in the District of Columbia. Gen. Carl "Tooey" Spaatz, formerly commander of U.S. Strategic Air Forces in Europe during the war, now commanding general of the Army Air Forces, outlined SAC's mission thusly,

The Strategic Air Command will be prepared to conduct long-range offensive operations in any part of the world either independently or in cooperation with land and naval forces; to conduct maximum-range reconnaissance over land or sea either independently or in cooperation with land and naval forces; to provide combat units capable of intense and sustained combat operations employing the latest and most advanced weapons; to train units and personnel for the maintenance of the Strategic Forces in all parts of the world; to perform such special missions as the Commanding General, Army Air Forces, may direct.

The assets of the Continental Air Forces were

Above: General George Kenney flew in from the Pacific to become SAC's first Commander in Chief.

divided among (in addition to SAC) the newly formed Tactical Air Command (TAC) and Air Defense Command (ADC), with SAC getting not only the former Continental Air Forces headquarters but the largest proportion of its other resources. These included the Second Air Force, based at Colorado Springs, the 311th Reconnaissance Wing, based at MacDill Field in Florida, as well as twenty-two other major and thirty minor bases. The personnel strength at these installations was listed at one hundred thousand, aircraft strength at thirteen thousand, but these numbers were declining dramatically due to demobilization. Ten days after the creation of SAC, on March 31, the Fifteenth Air Force, which

had been the backbone of the USAAF Strategic Air Offensive in the Mediterranean and southern Europe during the war (and which had been deactivated on September 15, 1945) was reactivated and assigned to SAC as a replacement for the Second Air Force, which was deactivated and assigned in inactive status to the Air Defense Command. The Fifteenth absorbed the staff of the Second and took as its headquarters the former home of the Second at Colorado Springs. The 311th Reconnaissance Wing, which had been assigned directly to SAC, became part of the Fifteenth Air Force on May 1.

On June 7, 1946, the Eighth Air Force, the largest and most famous of the USAAF Strategic Air Forces during the war, became part of SAC. The Eighth had been assigned to USAAF Pacific after the fall of Germany, and after moving Stateside as part of SAC, it was temporarily attached to the Fifteenth, for reasons of administration, between August 1 and November 1. As of November 19, the Eighth became operational at Fort Worth, Texas.

When SAC was established on March 21, 1946, the man tapped as its first commander in chief was the stocky, wiry-haired Gen. George Kenney, who had served under Gen. Douglas MacArthur in the Pacific as commander of the Allied Air Command and the U.S. Far East Air Forces (incorporating the Fifth and the Thirteenth Air Forces). In the meantime, however, Kenney had been assigned to temporary duty with the Military Staff Committee of the Joint Chiefs of Staff and later as senior American officer on the Military Staff Committee of the United Nations in London and later New York. With Kenney thus unavailable, the actual first commander of SAC was Maj. Gen. Saint Clair Streett, who had been appointed deputy commander on the day SAC was created. He was to serve as acting commander for SAC's first seven months until General Kenney reported for duty on October 15. Six days after General Kenney arrived, SAC officially relocated its headquarters from Bolling Field in the District of Columbia to Andrews Field, Maryland, eleven miles away.

Among the other units placed at SAC's disposal when it was created was the old 509th Composite Group of the 20th Air Force, the unit created for the purpose of dropping the atomic bombs on Japan. In mid-1946 the 509th was still the only unit capable of delivering nuclear weapons, and thus it was called upon to take part in Operation Crossroads, which would involve dropping a Nagasaki-type plutonium bomb on Bikini Atoll in the Pacific. The operation, authorized by the president in January, was designed to further study the effects of nuclear weapons. On July 1, 1946, the first nuclear bomb to be dropped by SAC fell from the bomb bay of the B-29 *Dave's Dream,* commanded by Maj. Woodrow P. Swancutt, into a cluster of ships anchored in the azure blue Pacific off Bikini.

While the creation and embryonic development of SAC was providing a cornerstone upon which a future would be built, demobilization was taking its toll. By the end of 1946 the personnel strength of the units assigned to SAC had been reduced by 63 percent to 37,092. SAC's aircraft strength had dropped by 78 percent in the nine months since its creation. The rosters listed only 279 aircraft—148 B-29s, 85 P-51s, and a handful of transport and reconnaissance aircraft. Of the nine bomb groups within SAC's numbered Air Forces, only six had aircraft assigned. Three existed only on paper.

By the time General Kenney arrived to head SAC, some of the complacency that had come with the demobilization had begun to erode. Tension between the Soviet Union and the other victorious powers had begun to increase. The Russians were busily establishing communist puppet states in the eastern European nations from which they had driven the Germans during

Above: Telephone operators on SAC's Operational Control System (SOCS).

the war. Face-offs got uglier, and a pair of USAAF transports were shot down over Yugoslavia. An American show of force was in order, but the enormous force that had defeated the Axis less than two years before no longer existed. The United States had almost nothing available that wasn't already in place in the occupation forces. But there were the B-29s, the giant Superfortresses, the only planes in the world capable of carrying the atomic bomb.

Six B-29s were rotated from Davis-Monthan Field, Arizona, to the Rhine-Main Airport near Frankfurt in the American zone of occupied Germany. The big bombers flew missions along the periphery of Soviet-occupied territory and surveyed airfields and airports throughout Western Europe for possible use by B-29s if World War III should come so soon after World War II. The postwar euphoria was gone, and the Cold War had arrived.

On September 18, 1947, Stuart Symington became the first secretary of the air force, and eight days later General Spaatz, then commanding general of the Army Air Forces, naturally became the first Chief of Staff of the USAF. General Kenney continued as commander of SAC. Between October and the end of 1947, SAC units underwent some basic changes. Under the Hobson reorganization plan, combat groups were taken from the jurisdiction of base commanders, who were frequently not fliers, and placed under a wing headquarters with the same numerical designation as the combat group. The wing commander rather than the base commander was

thus placed in the pivotal command position.

SAC ended 1947 with 713 aircraft, a 60 percent increase over the previous year. Of these, 319 were B–29s, more than double the number of the big bombers on hand in 1946. The number also included 230 F–51 piston-engined fighters and 120 F–80 jet fighters, earmarked as potential escorts for the bombers.

In 1948 SAC began to receive deliveries of the first of the enormous Convair B–36 strategic bombers. The B–36 was an outgrowth of the wartime desire for bigger and bigger bombers with longer and longer range. The B–29 had been a vast improvement over the aircraft flying in the

Above: Medical supplies are loaded aboard a B-36 at Carswell AFB for possible use during overseas training. SAC's insignia and blue band are particularly visible in this photo.

Left: An enormous B-36 and the fuel trucks required to feed it. The thirsty behemoths needed 21,116 gallons of fuel and 1200 gallons of oil.

early days of the war, and the B-36 would be the ultimate extension of the wartime thinking. Conceived during the war as a bomber capable of striking targets in Europe from bases in the United States and Canada, the big plane was not needed, because bases in England were never lost to the Germans. Thus the big bomber went on the back burner. With the end of the war and the growing Soviet threat, the idea of a huge bomber with intercontinental range took on increased importance. The plane, which first flew in August of 1946, was 40 percent larger than the B-29, with an 89-foot greater wing span, and a range of between six and seven thousand

miles, more than twice that of the B-29. The B-36 was the largest bomber ever in service, and although it has since been surpassed in performance, it has never been surpassed in size by any other bomber.

With the arrival of the B-36, the very heavy bomb groups—with their B-29s designated very heavy bombers—became medium bomb groups. Two groups were designated heavy bomb groups; one was fitted out with the first B-36s, and the other existed, because of budgetary limitations, only on paper. Twelve formerly very heavy, now medium, bomb groups shared by the end of the year 486 B-29s and 35 of the new Boeing B-50s, which were outwardly almost identical to B-29s but had a much improved overall structure, higher performance engines, and better range.

As the first B-36s were coming into the SAC arsenal, the lid of the coffin containing the corpse of the "Grand Alliance" that had defeated Hitler's Germany was finally and irrevocably sealed. After World War II, by way of the 1945 Berlin Four-Power Declaration, Germany had been partitioned into four occupation zones, with the city of Berlin, in the Russian zone, being divided into four zones as well. In June 1948 the Russians closed the borders of their zone to all ground transportation. Road and rail links between the Western zones of Germany and the Western zones of Berlin were cut. Communications and electricity were cut. The Russian intention was to drive its former allies out of Berlin and occupy the entire city. There were two million people in West Berlin who faced either Russian occupation or starvation. On June 26 the USAF decided on an airlift to relieve the blockaded city. Flying between Tempelhof Airport in the American sector of Berlin and several fields in the Western zones, USAF and, later, British transports began to airlift supplies to Berlin. Within two weeks the airlifters were averaging a landing every three minutes at Tempelhof, and they maintained that level until May 12, 1949, when the Russians lifted the blockade. In order to accomplish the airlift, the new Air Force brought in over three hundred C–54 transports from units all over the world, including not only those of the Military Air Transport Service, but those assigned to TAC and SAC as well.

When the blockade began, one B–29 squadron from the 301st Bomb Group was coincidentally at Fürstenfeldbruck in the American zone. SAC ordered the remainder of the 301st to deploy to Fürstenfeldbruck by way of Goose Bay, Labrador. By the end of the month, SAC had moved the 307th and 28th Bomb Groups to RAF bases in England. The B–29s were in place as a show of force only; it was the transports that did the work and brought about a successful and peaceful conclusion to the new USAF's first action.

SAC Headquarters

At one minute after midnight on November 9, 1948, the Strategic Air Command headquarters was permanently established at Offutt AFB, having been moved there from Andrews AFB outside Washington, D.C., over the course of the preceding weeks. Offutt AFB, nerve center for SAC's massive nuclear strike force, is strategically located in the center of the continent, thousands of miles from the vulnerable coastlines. It is eight miles south of Omaha, Nebraska, adjacent to the suburb of Bellevue, Nebraska, just across the Missouri River from Council Bluffs, Iowa. Situated on the Great Plains, 1,048 feet above sea level, the base comprises an area of 1,914 acres and employs 12,880 uniformed and 3,348 civilian personnel, with an annual payroll of over $300 million.

Activated in 1888, the base has been in continuous use since 1896, originally as the U.S. Army's Fort Crook. The fort, then the home of the 22d Infantry Regiment, is named for the famous Indian fighter Maj. Gen. George Crook, the man who tracked down and took the surrender of the notorious Apache guerrilla leader Geronimo. The first landing strip was constructed in 1921 as a refueling stop for cross-country mail flights. On May 6, 1924, the field was officially named in honor of an Omaha native, the young and dashing Lt. Jarvis Jennes Offutt, an Air Service flyer during World War I who died from injuries received when the aircraft he was flying from England to France crashed at Valheureux.

Between the world wars little aviation activity took place at Offutt Field, but in 1940 work began on a government aircraft factory and other facilities. The grass and clover landing field was paved and lengthened, and the factory began building the first of 1,585 Martin B–26 Marauder medium bombers. In 1943 production shifted to the giant Boeing B–29 Superfortress strategic bombers, of which 531 were produced at Offutt. Ironically (because SAC is today a nuclear strikeforce), among the B–29s produced here were the aircraft that would become *Enola Gay* and *Bock's Car,* the only two aircraft ever to deliver nuclear weapons in wartime. After the war, the factory closed, and Offutt Field became a reserve training center. In January 1948 Offutt Field, like all other existing Army airfields, became an air force base, and in November SAC headquarters moved into the former factory complex. Over the years the runway has been lengthened to 9,614 feet with a 1,000-foot overrun at each end. Between 1959 and 1965 Offutt was an Atlas ICBM site, but the Atlas missiles have since been deactivated.

Today the host unit at Offutt is SAC's 3902d Air Base Wing, providing administrative and logistical support for all the other units on the base as well as operating the seventy-five-bed Ehrling Bergquist USAF Regional Hospital and medical-dental facility. Units based at Offutt include the Military Airlift Command's Global Weather Central and 3d Weather Wing, providing worldwide weather reports to SAC and the JSTPS as well as all the major USAF commands. The Strategic Communications Division of the Air Force Communications Command is at Offutt, along with the 1st Aerospace Communications Group, providing electronic communications, data processing, and air traffic control support to SAC headquarters and the other units assigned to Offutt. The 4000th Satellite Operations Group at Offutt, familiarly known as "Four Grand," is in operational control of the Defense Meteorological Satellite Program. Britain's Royal Air Force maintains a detachment of its Strike Command at Offutt as a liaison with SAC and to support RAF aircraft that occasionally operate through the base. There are a number of other important units at Offutt, ranging from the 702d Air Force Band to the 6949th Electronic Security Group, but all the units in all the buildings across the sprawling complex are really there because of what goes on in Building 500, SAC Central, the control center for SAC's global alert forces.

8 LeMay Comes Aboard

The year 1948 was an important one for SAC. It was SAC's first full year as part of the independent USAF, and the Berlin blockade was SAC's first alert in the face of a serious world crisis. It was the first year that aerial refueling squadrons became operational in SAC, and it marked the move of SAC headquarters from Andrews AFB to Offutt AFB, where it has remained ever since. More important in terms of SAC's future development was the change of command. On October 15, General Kenney moved on to assume command of the Air University at Maxwell AFB, Alabama. Four days later Curtis Emerson LeMay, who had presided over the defeat of Japan as commander of the 21st Bomber Command and who, as commander of U.S. Air Forces in Europe, had organized the Berlin Airlift, became commander of the Strategic Air Command. LeMay's tenure was to last nearly a decade, longer than any other before or since, and LeMay would forever be part of SAC's legacy.

Curtis LeMay was a determined professional airman, a rising star in the new elite of Air Force officers who had received their baptism of fire in the skies over Germany and Japan. He was a stocky bull of a man, a hard worker who put in long hours and demanded the same of his men. His reputation for unsmiling ferocity stemmed partly from the fact that a severe sinus condition early in life had paralyzed the muscles in his face

63

to the extent that smiling was nearly impossible.

LeMay arrived from USAFE only a few days before SAC moved to Omaha. What he found was an appalling drop in the level of professionalism compared with the USAAF of three years earlier, entirely characteristic of how the entire USAF had been affected by demobilization. LeMay told of having found during a tour of a SAC base "a sergeant guarding a hangar with a ham sandwich." It made a colorful (albeit true) quote and was indicative of what LeMay would find throughout SAC. Demobilization had created widespread demoralization. Reenlistments were down, and that was cutting the heart out of SAC's cadre of veteran pilots.

When LeMay asked about the results of practice bombing drills, he was cheerily told that they were very good. Upon closer examination he discovered that the missions were being flown at moderate altitude so that the crews wouldn't have to bother with oxygen and that they were being flown against sonar reflectors anchored at sea. In his memoirs LeMay recalled, "There's not a single realistic mission being flown. Practically nothing in the way of training. Sorry shape? You can say that again."

LeMay's response was to order a maximum effort simulated bombing mission against Wright Field in Ohio. The result was what LeMay was to call the "darkest night in American military history." Not a single bomber was able to fly the mission as it had been briefed. LeMay was determined to turn SAC into the kind of command that could fulfill its mission, which was to mount a strategic air offensive when called upon. He organized a relentless training schedule. Everyone in SAC would be combat ready and know his job, whether job was to navigate a B–36 to Moscow or to cook meals for the crews.

Food service was one of LeMay's pet concerns. Napoleon realized that an army travels on its stomach, and LeMay knew that morale, efficiency, and ultimately, reenlistments and combat readiness depended on the quality of the food available to his men. He observed that the steaks served in the Air Force mess halls "could be traced to nearby shoe repair shops, the potatoes were being cooked in the base laundry, and that entomologists and herpetologists took a greater interest in the macaroni than did the men it was intended to feed."

LeMay quickly arranged some "combat training" for the SAC cooks. He put them on leave and to work in the kitchens of major hotels near their assigned bases. Soon they were learning how, as LeMay put it, "to make salad dressing out of something besides cough syrup and worm medicine; and not to slop the whole meal together when it was presented." Before long the work of SAC cooks was just as professional as the job being done by the combat crews.

LeMay, over the course of the first year and a half of his command, turned the flotsam of a chaotic demobilization into a first-rate, professional service. In retrospect, General LeMay had no harsh words for his predecessor. Indeed, he credited General Kenney with going a long way toward preventing a disastrous deterioration. He had held SAC together in its hand-me-down tar paper temporary USAAF buildings in the face of the dismantling of the services in the months following VJ Day.

LeMay began his shape-up of SAC units with the 509th, the most professional and most combat ready unit—the one that had dropped the atomic bombs. From the 509th he worked his way down into every nook and cranny of the SAC establishment. A typical B–36 training flight would involve the enormous bombers lumbering out of a base in Texas, flying over the icy blue North Pacific to the outer reaches of the Aleutians,

edging north across the Arctic Circle, then homeward through the turbulence of the mountains of southern Alaska and the spine of the Rockies. It would be a thirty-hour, seven thousand-mile mission, with the crew huddled in their aluminum cocoon plunging through darkness eight miles above the aurora borealis, over stark terrain that simulated the approach to Magnitogorsk, or Kuibyshev—or Moscow.

9 SAC in Korea

On the morning of June 25, 1950, the North Korean communists invaded South Korea to force reunification under a communist government. After World War II, Korea, then part of the Japanese Empire, had been stripped from Japan and divided into occupation zones among Russia and the Western powers, much as Germany had been. Separate governments, based on the model of the occupiers' own, were set up in the two Koreas, and ideological differences as they were, the two parts were never unified.

LeMay was awake the morning of the invasion before the Pentagon had come to life, studying SAC intelligence on strategic targets in North Korea. For the next two days, while word was not forthcoming from Washington, he was in contact with the commanders of SAC's numbered air forces. Gen. Emmett "Rosie" O'Donnell, commander of the Fifteenth Air Force, was flown to SAC headquarters.

On the ground the South Korean defenders

Above: B-29s at work in Korea. At left the camera records the point of impact as two North Korean railroad bridges are dropped on July 27, 1950. On the right, two strings of bombs plunge toward a snow-covered Pyongyang, on January 3, 1951.

were receiving a severe mauling. LeMay immediately proposed a strategic air offensive against North Korea. It would, he believed, halt the North Korean offensive and minimize casualties in the South. Washington refused to consider LeMay's suggestion. The response to the aggression of the North Koreans was to be a "police action," not a war. Unfortunately, the North Koreans did consider it a war. LeMay and the men in SAC saw early on what nearly everyone would see in retrospect—that the "police action" concept created a protracted war that filled MASH field hospitals with a great many dying and wounded Americans.

SAC did get the word to go, however, and they were ready. Four days after the command came from USAF Chief of Staff Hoyt Vandenberg, SAC

B–29s were over targets in North Korea. When factors like flying time, the need for staging through bases in Japan, and the international date line are taken into account, it was a pretty quick deployment. The only catch was that the strategic bombers were flying tactical missions against tactical targets. LeMay was furious. His B–29s were roaming the battle zone searching for targets of opportunity. In LeMay's words, they were "chasing tanks down mountain roads."

It didn't take long, however, for the Air Force to realize that there was merit in a strategic air offensive. A Far East Air Forces (FEAF) Bomber

67

Above: Beginning on August 10, 1950, B-29s began blasting the huge Wonsan Railroad Locomotive Works.

Command was established under General O'Donnell. Personnel, units, and B–29s were transferred directly from SAC, but not units with atomic capability. The remaining units, including the B–36-equipped units, stayed on alert at U.S. bases in case the Russians pulled what LeMay called the "Big Switch."

The bomber offensive opened in mid-July with a strike on the North Korean port of Wonsan and wound up at the end of September with the complete elimination of factories, railheads, and airfields in North Korea. United Nations forces under General MacArthur had by the end of November occupied all of North Korea. The Korean War, or rather, "police action," was expected to be successfully completed by Christmas. The communist Chinese, however, had other plans and suddenly entered the conflict en masse. The Chinese entry into the fray entirely changed the nature of things. With their overwhelming numbers they were able to push the U.N. forces back on a wide front. General MacArthur, commanding the U.N. forces, immediately requested air strikes north of the Yalu River against the staging areas in China. The massive tank parks and MiG bases would have been easy picking for O'Donnell's B–29s, and their destruction probably would have broken the back of the Chinese offensive. But the United States government, fearing that bombing China would provoke a wider war, even to the extent of involving the Russians, refused to permit raids above or near the Chinese border.

Now that all the strategic targets were immune from attack, the air war became entirely tactical. USAF and Navy fighter-bombers were employed against targets in those parts of North Korea that had been recaptured by the Chinese, while the new F–86 Sabre Jets dueled with MiGs in the skies over the battlefield. The B–29s that had remained behind were once again chasing tanks down mountain roads. The war was to continue for nearly three more years, chewing up thousands of American bodies, and it would end at almost the same place it started.

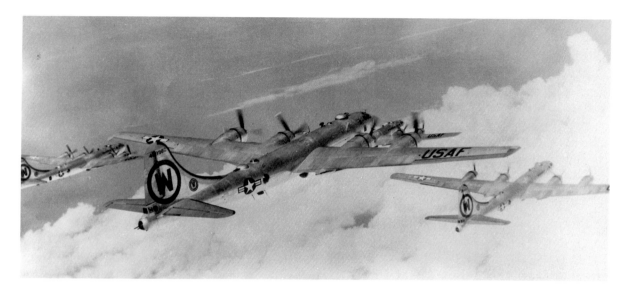

It is worth pointing out that the B–29 actions were not SAC's only contribution to the Korean conflict; SAC fighter escorts and tankers also took part. Throughout its first decade, and again briefly in 1958/59, SAC had included escort fighters in its inventory of aircraft. When the hostilities erupted, SAC had three fighter-escort wings equipped with Republic F–84s. In November 1950 the 27th FEW was sent to Japan (via aircraft carrier) to take up reconnaissance activities over Korea, where it served until August 1951— the only SAC fighter unit to serve in combat.

SAC had been experimenting for several years with in-flight refueling as a means of extending the range of its aircraft. In July SAC KB–29 tankers (converted from B–29 bombers) began the first aerial refueling missions under combat conditions. The tankers were assigned temporary duty with the 91st Strategic Reconnaissance Wing out of Yokota, Japan, and began service over North Korea refueling RF–80s and SAC RB–45s. It was a KB–29 of the 91st Strategic Reconnaissance Wing that was to fly the last combat mission in Korea on July 27, 1953.

Above: Eighth Air Force B-29 Superforts over Korea.

During the Korean War the FEAF Bomber Command was, with the exception of the 19th Bomb Wing, composed entirely of SAC units and commanded by SAC officers. FEAF Bomber Command B–29s and RB–29s flew 21,328 effective combat sorties, including 1,995 reconnaissance sorties and 797 psychological warfare sorties, with the B–29s dropping 167,000 tons of bombs on North Korean targets.

10 The Big Stick

The conflict in Korea has frequently been described as one that the United States fought with one hand tied behind its back. The hand that was tied was the one that held what Teddy Roosevelt would have called the Big Stick—the full weight of the Strategic Air Command. Throughout the war, while B–29s of World War II vintage flew their missions, SAC held back

Above: In the wake of a mid-winter blizzard, SAC ground crewmen prepare a B-47 Stratojet for a mission, circa 1955.

its B-36s and later, the world's first all-jet strategic bomber, Boeing's B-47 Stratojet.

Based on a mix of data from the highly sophisticated aeronautical think tanks of wartime Germany and Boeing's proven ability with advanced bombers (B-17 and B-29), the B-47 was committed to production in 1949. The first one of the sleek jets joined SAC in October 1951, when the Korean War was barely a year old. By the end of the war in 1953, SAC had 329 B-47s and 11 RB-47s (the reconnaissance version) in thirteen medium bomb wings, seven of which were completely equipped. This contrasted with six wings operating 110 B-29s and six heavy bomb wings operating 185 B-36s.

The B-36 and B-47 were unique airplanes for their time, the former being the largest bomber in the world, the latter being the only jet bomber. Between them they provided SAC with unprecedented range, bomb capacity, and speed. They were Curtis LeMay's Big Stick, technologically leaps and bounds ahead of what SAC was fielding in Korea. SAC was feverishly building up an arsenal of the most technologically advanced weapons systems. The B-36 arsenal reached

Above: SAC's arsenal once included fighters, with its F-84s serving in Korea.

its peak in 1954 with 342 of the huge planes (133 were RB–36 variants) in service. Between 1956 and 1959, SAC averaged between 1,500 and 1,560 B–47s and RB–47s, more than any other type of bomber since the Second World War. With these aircraft, and their nuclear weapons capability, the American strategic arsenal of the mid-fifties had a clear and unprecedented superiority. Carefully constructed by Curtis LeMay, this military might was held in readiness to counteract a full-scale Soviet attack, not intended for use in the Korean War.

This was the concept of deterrence. After the Soviet detonation of a nuclear device in 1949,

the real threat of a "nuclear Pearl Harbor" became a guiding force in the formulation of American strategic policy. The Soviet sneak attack, it was theorized, could be prevented if the Russians knew their attack would result in a counterattack of greater magnitude. It is a coincidence, or perhaps a case of cause and effect, that the B–36 and B–47 were brought into service, served operationally, and phased out without ever being flown on a wartime bombing mission.

In 1955 SAC took delivery of the first 744 of what would become probably the most famous strategic bomber to see service in the forty years since World War II. Boeing's B–52 Stratofortress was an eight-engine, all-jet heavy bomber designed to replace the B–36. It was originally intended to serve as SAC's first-line bomber for maybe a decade, then to be replaced by another aircraft, as the B–36 had replaced the B–29 and the B–52 was now replacing the B–36. Due to a variety of factors, among them that the Boeing people had designed and built a truly outstanding airplane, the B–52 is, thirty years later, still SAC's first-line bomber.

SAC Aircraft Strength (Excluding Bombers)

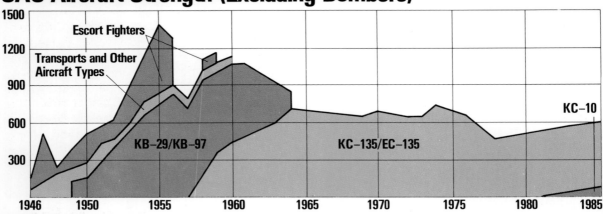

SAC Bomber Strength

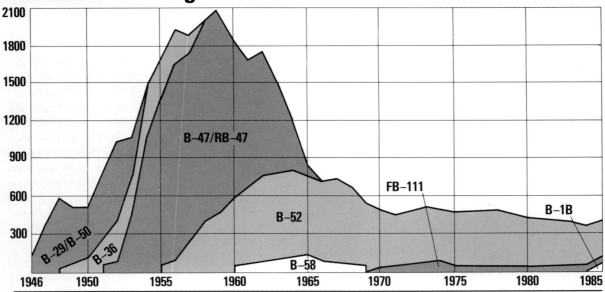

The B–47 and B–36 were products of an era when jet engines did not have the fuel efficiency required for a long-range heavy bomber. Hence, the B–36, driven primarily by six turboprop engines (with jet engines for added speed and power when needed), remained as SAC's long-range heavy bomber, while the all-jet B–47, with shorter range, was classed as a medium bomber. The problem was the amount of fuel that could be carried. In order to carry enough fuel to achieve the range of a B–36, an all-jet bomber built with late forties–early fifties technology would have had to be an enormous, unwieldy, unmaneuverable fuel tank.

The answer to the problem was to be the B–52, with its eight Pratt & Whitney J57 turbojets developing up to 10,000 pounds of thrust in each. The new bomber was a foot shorter and had a wingspan 45 feet less than the B–36 but was 51 feet longer and 69 feet wider than Boeing's earlier B–47. The B–52's range of 7,500 miles matched or exceeded all models of B–36 and was double that of the B–29 and B–47. The final B–52 model series, the TF33 turbofan-powered B–52H, had a designated range of 10,000 miles. (On January 11, 1962, a B–52H set the distance record for nonrefueled aircraft by flying 12,532 miles in twenty-two hours and nine minutes. The record still stands.)

On June 29, 1955, SAC's first B–52 was flown to Castle AFB, California, from the Boeing factory in Seattle, by Brig. Gen. William E. Eubank, commander of the 93d Bomb Wing, based at Castle.

On January 16, 1957, three B–52s took off from Castle on an operation called Power Flite. Over the course of the next forty-five hours and nineteen minutes, the three bombers flew *nonstop* around the world. It was less than half the time required for the first nonstop round-the-world flight, by a SAC B–50, *Lucky Lady II,* in 1949. The commander of the lead aircraft, *Lucky Lady III,* was Lt. Col. James Morris, who had been the co-pilot of *Lucky Lady II* during her nonstop flight in 1949. The flight was commanded by Maj. Gen. Archie Old, commander of the Fifteenth Air Force. In addition to the three primary aircraft in Power Flite, there were two spares, one of them dropping out as planned at RAF Brize Norton in England and the other dropping out in Labrador because of a refueling problem at the first aerial refueling point. The three primary aircraft went on to be refueled in-flight over North Africa, the Indian Ocean, and the Pacific, by KB–97 aerial tankers. The flight plan called for the lead aircraft to land at the Fifteenth Air Force headquarters at March AFB in Southern California, with the other two returning to Castle. Castle was, however, socked in by the thick tule fog common in California's Central Valley in the winter, so all three aircraft set down at March, within two minutes of the scheduled arrival time. The three crews were greeted by General LeMay, who awarded each man the Distinguished Flying Cross and called the flight a "demonstration of SAC's capabilities to strike any target on the face of the earth."

11 The Changing of the Guard

On July 1, 1957, Curtis LeMay left his job as commander in chief of SAC to become Vice Chief of Staff of the Air Force. He was replaced by Gen. Thomas S. Power, who had been LeMay's vice commander between 1948 and 1954 and had been commander of the Air Research and Development Command between 1954 and 1957. During LeMay's nine-year tenure with the Strategic Air Command, SAC had risen from a personnel strength of 51,965 to 224,014, an increase of over 400 percent. Aircraft strength had risen from 837 planes to 2,711. More than half of the heavy bomb wings were equipped with B–52s, over two hundred in all. In 1948 when LeMay took over, SAC had twenty-one bases in the continental United States. In 1957 LeMay turned over to Power thirty-eight Stateside and thirty overseas bases, including bases in Puerto Rico, the United Kingdom, North Africa, Spain, Greenland, Newfoundland, Labrador, and Guam. LeMay had presided over the buildup of the most potent strategic bomber force

in history, but Power's tenure would see the Strategic Air Command enter an entirely new era. Power took command of SAC when it had 1,895 bombers and but a single unequipped strategic missile squadron. When he left in 1964, on the eve of the Vietnam War, SAC would have 1,206 bombers and 931 intercontinental ballistic missiles.

Curtis LeMay had built SAC into a first-class fighting machine with state-of-the-art equipment. But state-of-the-art is, by definition, a transitory condition, and there had to be in place a system for continually updating SAC's arsenal. Among SAC's goals in the late fifties and early sixties was the phase-out of the B–47 and the B–36 as first-line bombers, the phase-in of the B–52, and the beginning of a search for the eventual successor to the B–52. With supersonic interceptors standard equipment with most of the world's major air forces, particularly that of the Soviet Union, the bomber of the future would certainly have to have a speed in excess of Mach 1. Various means of propulsion were also being discussed.

A great deal of research and development money had been diverted into a top secret project to develop a nuclear-powered aircraft. Nuclear propulsion had a lot of advantages. A teaspoon of fuel would give an aircraft the range to fly several times around the world. The Navy was building a fleet of nuclear-powered submarines and was planning nuclear-powered surface ships. It seemed to be the wave of the future. General Spaatz had predicted that nuclear-powered aircraft would be in service by the seventies.

Nuclear propulsion, however, had some rather thorny disadvantages. First, there was the problem of the weight of the reactor; then there was the problem of the shielding required to protect the crew from radiation. The combined weight of the power plant alone was many tons more than any existing aircraft. The Navy could build ships large enough to carry both reactors and radia-

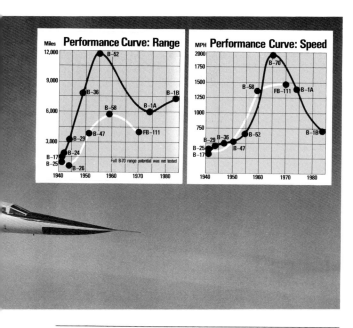

Performance Curve: Range

Performance Curve: Speed

Above: The North American B-70 Valkyrie with a Convair B-58, its weapons pod clearly visible, in the background. The Mach 3 B-70 at 170 feet was 77 feet longer than the Mach 2 B-58.

tion shields, but it was eventually proven technically impossible to build a nuclear-powered aircraft, especially one that could fly faster than the speed of sound. Beyond these technical limitations, the advances being made in aerial refueling made limited range less a problem than it had been.

Thus it came to be that the supersonic successor to the B-52 was a product of the evolution of conventional jet propulsion. The B-58 Hustler, first flown in November of 1956, was the world's first supersonic bomber and the first to exceed Mach 2. The B-58 was slightly shorter than a B-29 or B-47, but its highly swept, delta-wing surfaces were only 57 feet tip to tip. It was a thin, sleek ship with the bomb load carried externally in an equally streamlined weapons pod that was roughly two thirds the size of the plane's

fuselage. Thus, once the payload was dropped, the plane became a good deal smaller, faster, and more maneuverable, all the better to effect an exit from the target area. The B-58 was built by Convair (formerly Consolidated-Vultee, now General Dynamics), the same contractor that had been responsible for the B-36 and, before that, the B-24 of World War II fame.

The first USAF Hustlers were delivered to the Air Research and Development Command in 1959, and on August 1, 1960, the first twelve became operational with SAC's 43d Bomb Wing at Carswell AFB, Texas. On January 12, 1961, a 43d Bomb Wing B-58 piloted by Maj. Henry Deutschendorf established six international speed and payload records, five of them previously held by the Soviet Union. Staging out of Edwards AFB, California, the B-58 flew 1,200 mph with a 2000-kilogram, a 1000-kilogram and a zero payload over a distance of 1000 kilometers. With the same payloads, the plane flew a distance of 2000 kilometers at 1,061.808 mph. Two days later another 43d Bomb Wing B-58 commanded by Maj. Harold Confer established three new records for the 1000-kilometer course with a speed of 1,284.73 mph, winning the 1961 Thompson Trophy. On May 10, Maj. Elmer Murphy's B-58 established a record for sustained speed, flying 669.4 miles in thirty minutes forty-five seconds at an average speed of 1,302 mph. For his flight, Murphy received the Bleriot Cup from the Aero Club of France.

Two weeks later, another B-58, commanded by Maj. William Payne, flew the 4,612 miles from New York to Paris in three hours nineteen minutes, one tenth the time taken by Charles Lindbergh for his famous 1927 flight. On the third of June, however, the same plane with the same crew crashed while participating in the Paris Air Show, killing those aboard.

On March 5, 1962, two months after a SAC B-52 had established a new unrefueled dis-

tance record of 12,532 miles, another 43d BW B–58, commanded by Capt. Robert Sowers, made a round-trip flight between Los Angeles and New York in four hours forty-one minutes. Despite the need to decelerate to subsonic speed for in-flight refueling, the aircraft beat the sun across the continent on the return flight, and averaged 1,214.65 mph. The following year, in Operation Greased Lightning, a B–58 of the 305th Bomb Wing at Bunker Hill AFB, Indiana, set a Tokyo–London speed record, flying the route in eight hours thirty-five minutes. In March 1964 after the disastrous Alaska earthquake, the 43d Bomb Wing was asked to make a high-priority reconnaissance flight over the area. Two B–58s were on the way two hours later, and twelve hours

Above: A tail-gun-equipped B-58 begins its take-off roll; while *(inset)* a B-52 flys a low-level mission over the Northwest Coast.

after their takeoff the processed photographs were ready for viewing in Washington.

In December 1965, despite its having established itself as the fastest strategic bomber in history, with more records than any other com-

bat aircraft, the phaseout of the B–58 was announced by Secretary of Defense Robert McNamara. The B–58 phaseout was part of a controversial reduction in the SAC bomber force that would involve base closures and retirement of early model B–52s as well as all of the B–58 fleet. The last B–36 had been withdrawn from service a year before the first B–58 arrived, the last B–47 was gone when the B–58 phaseout was announced five years later, and the last of the 116 B–58s was quietly retired in 1970, leaving the B–52 as SAC's only bomber. It is ironic that, even as its supersonic "successor" was disappearing into mothballs, the B–52 was up to its armpits in combat in America's costliest war. Of SAC's four great postwar strategic bombers, only one, the B–52, was ever involved in combat.

The reasons for the demise of the B–58 are still not fully clear. The B–36 and B–47 were clearly objects of the past when they left SAC, but why retire the world's fastest production strategic bomber? Some say it was politics, and there are the pragmatists who say it was the cost of maintaining an expensive weapons system whose function could be largely duplicated by other aircraft. The most often repeated reason was that the B–58 was designed for high-altitude operations, and by the late sixties Soviet air defenses had become effective at high altitude. The latter is questionable, because the B–52, also designed for high-altitude operations, was successfully adapted for low-level operations. Indeed, improvements in Soviet air defenses were evident when, in November 1959, SAC and the Federal Aviation Agency jointly announced the establishment of seven special air routes (20 miles by 500 miles) over which SAC bombers would fly low-level training missions. Furthermore, the 1964 Alaska earthquake reconnaissance missions had been flown at low level by B–58s. In the end it was probably a

combination of many reasons, both real and perceived, that caused the B–58 to slip from SAC inventory.

When you draw a performance curve for medium bombers from the World War II mediums, such as the B–25 and B–26, through the B–29 (which was, as we've seen, downgraded from "very heavy" to "medium" when dwarfed by the B–36), through the B–47, you arrive at the B–58. When you draw a performance curve for heavy bombers from the World War II heavies, such as the B–17 and B–24, through the B–29, through the B–36, and through the B–52, you arrive at a space that would be occupied by a bomber of enormous size, flying at more than twice the speed of sound.

Such a plane actually came to exist. It was North American's B–70, and it reached a higher peak on the performance curve than any other bomber ever had or ever would. With a length of 185 feet, the delta-winged behemoth was more than 20 feet longer than either the B–36 or B–52, but at the widest point, the tail, the wingspan was a trim 105 feet, just over half the span of the earlier heavy bombers.

The sleek, arrow-shaped ship was the crest of the aviation technology boom that began during World War II. The B–70 was designed to cruise

at, not twice, but three times, the speed of sound! Operating at Mach 3, the bomber would be flying several hundred miles per hour faster than any existing interceptor. Design work on the B–70 began in 1956, in the hands of the same generation of scientists that would take astronauts to the moon. North American Aviation received a $360 million contract to develop the airframe, and General Electric's engine division got $115 million to develop what would be the 31,000-pound thrust YJ–93 engine, six of which would push the 250-ton B–70 to a service ceiling of over 70,000 feet. The plane's designers were breaking new ground in aircraft design. New materials were being fashioned to construct an aircraft that would cope with the 650-degree heat generated on the leading edges during Mach 3 flight. The results of their work earned the B–70 engineers an "Advancement of Research" award from the American Society of Metals. The fuselage was designed to have the same shape as the shock wave it would generate at Mach 3. In this way, the aircraft would take advantage of "compression lift" by using its own shock wave to increase its forward velocity.

In the dozen years since World War II, there had been more different types of experimental high-performance aircraft than there would be in

the next thirty years. When the ground was broken for North American's big B–70 plant at Palmdale, California, nobody realized that this plane would be at the top of the performance curve. And nobody realized that the school of thought that had created the performance curve had turned around. Strategic thinking was turning to missiles. Weapons systems' costs were being glowered at by Congress. A new era of lowered expectations was dawning on the airplane industry.

In December 1959, only eight months after it had given the go-ahead, the Department of Defense reversed itself and downgraded the B–70 program from a production bomber program to a test program in which only two prototype XB–70s would be built. The first prototype XB–70 (tail number 20001) first flew on September 21, 1964, and the test-flight schedule began. The two prototypes would be test-flown to research the effects of supersonic flight on so huge an airframe. The B–70 was the largest aircraft to fly faster than sound, and it was designed to fly faster than any other supersonic aircraft. By the following spring the XB–70s were routinely cruising at Mach 3 for periods of nearly an hour.

Then disaster struck. On June 8, 1965, the second prototype XB–70 (20207) was high over

Above: The last flight of XB-70 20207 on June 8, 1966. Walker's Starfighter, just to the right of the B-70 in the first picture, is a ball of flame in the second. Its vertical tail surfaces torn off by the Starfighter, the B-70 continued momentarily in level flight (second picture), then rolled out of control (third), and crashed into the desert (last).

the Mojave Desert being escorted by four smaller jets for a picture-taking session conducted by General Electric's engine division, which had built the engines for the five aircraft. At the controls were the veteran B–70 test pilot Al White and Maj. Carl Cross, a newcomer to the B–70 program but a pilot who had logged 8,530 hours, many of them in combat. Just behind the XB–70's starboard wing was a Lockheed F–104 piloted by Joe Walker, a highly regarded test pilot who held the world's speed record for his 4,100 mph flight in the X–15 rocket plane. At 9:24 A.M. the tail of Walker's plane clipped the big bomber's wingtip. In an instant the F–104 flipped over and was literally dragged across the top of the XB–70's wings, virtually destroying both of the big plane's rudders. As the photographer, hovering nearby in a Lear Jet, recorded the event, Walker's plane disintegrated into a ball of fire.

The XB–70 continued in perfect, level flight for sixteen seconds, then suddenly threw itself to the right and went into a violent end-over-end

tumble that ended 25,000 feet below in the Mojave Desert. Walker died instantly. White managed to eject and, though severely injured when the ejection capsule malfunctioned, he survived the crash. Cross was still alive and fighting to get into his ejection capsule when White punched out, but he ultimately rode the doomed bird to his death.

The remaining XB–70 prototype ended up in static display at the Air Force Museum. The project that had produced the world's fastest bomber wound down without ever delivering an operational aircraft to a SAC wing. Ironically, the Russians went on to build the world's fastest interceptor, the MiG-25 Foxbat, *because* of the B–70.

North American Aviation became a division of Rockwell International and ultimately built the space shuttle. Twenty years after the B–70 first flew, North American/Rockwell began delivering to SAC its first new strategic bomber since the B–58, the B–1B. With a final twist of irony, it should be noted that the B–1B will cruise at less than a third the cruising speed of the B–70.

12 SAC Missile Forces

Intercontinental ballistic missiles, which entered SAC service in September 1959, added an awesome and fearsome new dimension to strategic warfare. Adversaries could now strike one another with nuclear blows while their personnel remained thousands of miles apart. SAC had first gotten into the missile business in March 1956, when Headquarters USAF gave SAC and the Air Research and Development Command

missiles (IRBMs). By that time the Navy was planning for integration of submarine-launched ballistic missiles (SLBMs) into its fleet of nuclear subs, and SAC was beginning to plan for such supersonic ICBMs as Atlas and Titan.

In May 1957 Patrick AFB, Florida, was selected as the first Snark missile training base. The 556th Strategic Missile Squadron activated there in December, but the first launch wasn't to take place until the following June. The Snark was SAC's first missile, having been chosen over the air-breathing Navajo missile, whose development was terminated. The small Rascal and Goose were also canceled as emphasis drifted toward development of the Snark and the larger Thor IRBM and Atlas ICBM, as well as the U.S. Army–developed Jupiter IRBM. SAC's involvement in the Jupiter program was in line with Secretary Wilson's earlier directive.

By 1958 strategic missiles had developed to the point where they could start the transition from research and development status to operational status. In January the 1st Missile Division at Vandenberg AFB was transferred from the Air Force Research and Development Command to SAC. The 576th and 704th Strategic Missile Squadrons were assigned the task of becoming operational with the Atlas, the first SAC ICBM, and functioning as a training ground for further Atlas-equipped units. The 1st Missile Division also assumed control of the first Titan ICBM unit, the 703d Strategic Missile Wing, based at Lowry AFB, Colorado.

On September 9, 1959, the first Atlas missile, an Atlas D, was launched by the 576th Strategic Missile Squadron from a pad at Vandenberg AFB. The big, 75-foot missile traveled over four thousand miles downrange at a speed of 16,000 mph, and was powered by Rp–1 liquid propellant and liquid oxygen. By year's end, six Atlas, along with thirteen Snark, missiles were on active alert on open launch pads at Vandenberg.

Above: A gleaming B-58 racing into the gathering twilight. Once the fastest bomber in the world, the B-58's own twilight would come all too soon.

the responsibility for developing an initial operational capability with the Thor missile, which SAC would deploy in England in cooperation with the Royal Air Force. In July SAC initiated plans for a broad series of strategic missiles. These included, in addition to Thor, the Snark and Navajo subsonic intercontinental missiles, as well as Goose, Rascal, and Quail, which were designed to be air-launched—precursors of the air-launched cruise missile (ALCM) of the 1980s.

In a November 1956 memo clarifying the roles of the various services Secretary of Defense Charles E. Wilson gave the Air Force sole responsibility for the development and deployment of ground-launched intercontinental ballistic missiles (ICBMs) and intermediate-range ballistic

By 1961, deployment of the Thor IRBMs to England had been completed; sixty-two Atlas D and Atlas E ICBMs were on alert with seven strategic missile squadrons, and squadrons were being formed to accept the more powerful Titan I and Minuteman I when they came on line. The Minuteman was originally designed as, and had been tested as, a mobile-launched missile. During the summer of 1960, a modified test train traveled across various railroad routes in the western and central sections of the United States to study such factors as the ability of the nation's railroads to support mobile missile trains, the probable effect on sensitive missiles and launch equipment, as well as the human factors involved in the operation. In his special defense budget message of March 28, 1961, President John Kennedy announced that the Mobile Minuteman concept would be abandoned in favor of basing the missiles in hardened underground silos. In the same message, Kennedy announced that the Snark missile, which he called "obsolete and of marginal military value," would be phased out just as it had become operational.

On December 11, 1961, less than a year after assuming office, Secretary of Defense Robert McNamara set the direction that SAC would follow for the following dozen years. "The introduction of ballistic missiles," said McNamara, "is already exerting a major impact on the size, composition, and deployment of the manned

bomber force, and this impact will become greater in the years ahead. As the number of . . . ballistic missiles increases, requirements for strategic aircraft will be gradually reduced. Simultaneously, the growing enemy missile capability will make grounded aircraft more vulnerable to sudden attack, and further readiness measures will have to be taken to increase the survivability rate of the strategic bomber force."

SAC had thirty-eight strategic missile squadrons in its arsenal by the end of 1963, armed with 631 ICBMs and IRBMs, including 119 Titan I and II, and 372 Minuteman I. In addition, the arsenal held nearly 1,100 Hound Dog and Quail air-launched missiles. Throughout the sixties, successive administrations in Washington, building on the cornerstone laid in 1961 by Secretary

Above: The Titan ICBM silo is protected from enemy attack by enormous steel and concrete doors weighing 200 tons.

McNamara, held to the school of thought that the huge ICBMs would eclipse, not only the manned bomber, but a whole lineage of conventional weaponry in the brick wall of the nation's strategic deterrent. During that decade, while the number of Minuteman ICBMs grew from one to over a thousand and the number of strategic bombers fell from 1,735 to 549, the Department of Defense technocrats were getting themselves deeply embroiled in an increasingly sticky brushfire war in a faraway place. The war in Vietnam would teach a new generation of strategic planners a great number of lessons about strategic policy.

Part IV
SAC in Southeast Asia

13 Dreaming of a "Sub-limited War"

The strategic thinking that was percolating to the top in the defense department in the early sixties was starting to sound strangely similar to what had come on the heels of World War II. Under a nuclear umbrella held aloft by an arsenal of ICBMs, conventional weaponry would be obsolete. The scheme had already cost SAC the B–58 and the B–70, and the B–52 was soon to follow. But even as the theoreticians in the Pentagon were confidently working out the calculations that would peel serious conventional warfare from the nation's future like a kid removing a Band-Aid, they were also planning for what they would come to call "sub-limited war", or a war in which the nation's most potent weapons and tactics would not be used.

In faraway Indochina just such a war was beginning to crackle into life. North Vietnam, supported by the Russians and the Chinese, was supplying antigovernment rebel movements in both South Vietnam and Laos. Nobody in the Kennedy administration wanted to see two more countries slip behind the bamboo curtain, and Secretary of Defense Robert McNamara took an interest in the conflict, seeing it as a "laboratory for the development of organizations and procedures for the conduct of sub-limited war."

In 1961 the U.S. Army's elite Special Forces, in their distinctive green berets, were sent into South Vietnam to help train the South Vietnamese in the conduct of sub-limited war. By the end of the year the Air Force was there as well. A combat unit of "air commandos" flying aging prop planes was sent in to help train the fledgling South Vietnamese Air Force (VNAF). By the end of 1962, it was becoming clear that the communist guerrillas did not view the war as sub-limited anymore than the North Koreans had viewed the conflict a dozen years earlier as a police action. The need for air support was exceeding the limited ability of the VNAF, so Americans began flying combat missions in armed T–28s and old World War II vintage B–26s.

It had become abundantly evident that the materiel and staging base for the guerrillas was North Vietnam. Curtis LeMay, now Chief of Staff of the Air Force, and many others, Chief of Naval Operations Adm. David McDonald and Marine Corps Commandant Gen. Wallace Green included, felt that a concentrated strategic air offensive against North Vietnam would be decisive in ending the war at the enemy's source of supply. On the other side of the fence were Secretary McNamara and the chairman of the Joint Chiefs of Staff, Army Gen. Maxwell Taylor, who advocated fighting the war exclusively in the South after enemy supplies had been delivered.

Left: B-52Ds on an Arc Light raid over Vietnam, December 1966.

85

The conflict came to a head at the June 1964 strategy conference in Honolulu, where it was decided that Vietnam would be an Army war with a tactical, but not strategic, role for airpower.

Scarcely more than two months later, on August 2 and again on August 4, North Vietnamese patrol boats attacked the U.S. Navy destroyers *Maddox* and *C. Turner Joy* in the Gulf of Tonkin off North Vietnam. President Johnson asked for and received from Congress authorization to launch air attacks against North Vietnam in retaliation for the attacks on the ships. The authorization came in the form of what came to be known as the Gulf of Tonkin Resolution. With it, the United States stepped across the threshold into what would start as limited retaliation (sub-limited war?) but would become the longest war in American history.

In July 1965, almost a year after the Gulf of Tonkin, Curtis LeMay retired as Air Force Chief of Staff. He had this to say about Vietnam:

All along I said that if we were going to get anywhere in Vietnam, we'd have to attack the North. But voices have been saying repeatedly, "No, we must recognize a stable government, down there in the South, before we dare carry the war to the North." I don't believe that. If you carry the war to the North and really carry it there, you'll get your stable government.

The military task confronting us is to make it so expensive for the North Vietnamese that they will stop their aggression against South Vietnam and Laos. If we make it too expensive for them, they will stop. They don't want to lose everything they have. There came a time when the Nazis threw the towel into the ring. Same way with the Japanese. We didn't bring that happy day about by sparring with sixteen-ounce gloves.

My solution to the problem would be to tell them frankly that they've got to draw in their horns and stop their aggression or we're going to bomb them back into the Stone Age with airpower or naval power—not with ground forces.

You could tell them this. But they might not be convinced that you really meant business. What you must do with those characters is to convince them that if they continue their aggression, they will have to pay an economic penalty which they cannot afford. We must throw a punch that really hurts.

Successful prosecution of this war would not necessarily require introduction of nuclear weapons. But you won't get anywhere until you really swat the communists. This could be done with conventional weapons.

Maxim: Apply whatever force it is necessary to employ to stop things quickly. The main thing is stop it. The quicker you stop it, the more lives you save.

14 SAC Goes to War

SAC's role in the Vietnam War began as one of support. In November 1961 Headquarters USAF had designated SAC as the single manager of all KC–135 air-refueling operations, and as such SAC would provide air-refueling support for fighter and other aircraft operated by all other major USAF commands. SAC tankers were used to support combat operations for the first time on June 9, 1964, when four KC–135s, code-named Yankee Team Tanker Task Force, operating out of Clark AB in the Philippines, re-fueled eight F–100 fighters on a mission over Laos. After the initial mission the Yankee Team tankers were rotated back to Andersen AFB on Guam where they resumed routine operations. After the Gulf of Tonkin incident, the Yankee Team tankers were sent back to Clark. Re-named Foreign Legion on September 8, the tankers began supporting Pacific Air Forces

(PACAF) fighters in combat operations on September 28.

SAC's entry into the refueling scene coincided with the grounding of PACAF's own tankers. PACAF had for years been using the tanker version of the old B–50 bomber, the KB–50. PACAF had rotated these old birds to forward fighter bases in Southeast Asia from home bases in Japan. In October, after a KB–50 crashed, a fleetwide inspection turned up a significant level of deterioration in the aircraft, and they were retired. Suddenly SAC's KC–135s found themselves with responsibility for all refueling operations in the Far East and the Southeast Asia war zone. Kadena AB, Okinawa, was selected as the SAC KC–135 home base, with Don Muang Airport, Thailand, as the forward base. On January 12, 1965, the 4252d Strategic Wing was activated at Kadena, and by the end of the month the Thailand-based tankers were supporting PACAF tactical aircraft in the war zone. The Kadena-based tanker operations were designated Young Tiger, while Foreign Legion was

Above: A rare photo of an RB-47 on the flight line at Tan Son Nhut AB, South Vietnam, in April 1966 as a fuel dump burns in the background. The B-47 never went to war as a bomber, but the recon version had several close scrapes including the 1961 shooting down of an RB-47 by the Russians.

rotated from Clark to Don Muang under the designation Tiger Cub. Meanwhile, PACAF's 2d Air Division (later Seventh Air Force), responsible for all tactical air operations in Southeast Asia except Navy and SAC aircraft, was located at Tan Son Nhut Airport near Saigon. SAC established a liaison office at Tan Son Nhut, known as SACLO, to coordinate refueling operations.

The United States finally began an organized air offensive against North Vietnam in March 1965, under the code name Rolling Thunder. But the aircraft were tactical, and so were the targets. The former included F–100 and F–105 fighter-bombers under 2d Air Division control, supported by the SAC tankers already in place in Thailand.

Meanwhile, a decision had been made to commit the awesome firepower of SAC's bomb-

Left: A SAC B-52D passes over a partially completed Buddhist temple near U Tapao Royal Thai Navy Air Base as it thunders out on an Arc Light mission over South Vietnam.

Above: SAC armorers load bombs on a B-52 at U Tapao.

ers. The targets, however, would not be strategic targets in the North, but tactical targets in South Vietnam. Both B–47 and B–52 wings were ordered to prepare to go to war. They would be based at Andersen AFB on Guam and would conduct raids on Vietcong jungle hideouts under the code name Arc Light. It would be the first application in actual combat of either of the Boeing bombers. On the eve of their deployment, however, the B–47s, older and shorter of range, were deleted from the roster and the big B–52s set out across the wide Pacific alone, bound for the war zone and for a whole new chapter in SAC's history.

The much-heralded first B–52 combat mission on June 18, 1965, was less than a success. The American press compared it to "swatting flies with a sledgehammer"; results on the ground were near nil, and two of the big planes were lost in a midair collision in the refueling area. Despite all of this, U.S. Army Gen. William Westmoreland, commander of U.S. forces in Vietnam, felt that Arc Light had potential and supported its continuation. Through the end of 1965, Guam-based B–52s of the 7th, 320th, and 454th Bomb Wings flew over one hundred missions to Vietnam. Most of the missions were simply saturation bombing, but in the fall, the B–52s, like the

B-29s in Korea, turned to tactical support missions in support of the U.S. Marine Corps Operation Harvest Moon and the U.S. Army First Cavalry operations in the Ia Drang Valley.

The B-52s were being used simply as aerial artillery; they were giant bombing platforms. Suspended high above their targets, they were neither seen nor heard on the ground until the bombs struck. While the B-52 crews flew their tedious routine missions against the unseen, unheard targets in the South, tactical aircraft of PACAF's Seventh Air Force (upgraded from 2d Air Division on April 1, 1966) were striking targets in North Vietnam. Far from being strategic targets, the target selection process specifically and purposely excluded anything that was not directly associated with the movement of troops and materiel to the South or that posed an immediate threat to the aircraft involved. Rolling Thunder, as directed by Secretary McNamara, was a limited application of tactical airpower. While McNamara was still operating under the notion of a limited war, the North Vietnamese were pouring supplies into South Vietnam and building at home the most elaborate air defense system in the history of warfare.

To stop the infiltration with airpower would require destroying the railyards and marshaling yards in the Hanoi-Haiphong area (off-limits because they were strategic targets) or attempting to destroy the Ho Chi Minh Trail, that incredible labyrinth of jungle roads and trails leading north to south via Laos. The Ho Chi Minh Trail was invisible from the air because of the jungle and virtually impossible to destroy because there were almost no natural choke points. Bombed bridges could be repaired or, more easily, bypassed. Among the choke points that did exist were the passes that led from southern North Vietnam through the mountains to the jungles of Laos. One of the most important was the Mu Gia Pass, about sixty-five miles south of the North Viet-

namese city of Vinh. It was against Mu Gia Pass on April 12 and 26, 1966, that the B-52s first went North.

By June, after a year in the war zone, B-52s were dropping 8000 tons of bombs monthly in saturation raids on South Vietnam, both day and night and in all kinds of weather. The B-52s, because they flew too high to be seen or heard until too late, were gradually becoming the most feared weapon of the war. General Westmoreland put it best when he said, "We know, from talking to many prisoners and defectors, that the enemy troops fear B-52s, tactical air, artillery, and armor . . . in that order."

As a species of plant or animal, finding itself exiled to an unfamiliar environment, learns to adapt, so too did the B-52s. The B-52, as we've seen, was designed to carry nuclear weapons, which compress a vast amount of destructive power into a relatively compact space. Consequently, the bomb bay of the B-52 had a capacity of only twenty-seven conventional 500- or 750-pound bombs. When Arc Light began, SAC committed to battle its fleet of B-52Fs, the newest of the nearly identical B-52A through F series of models that made up most of the B-52 production run. At the same time, SAC reserved the more sophisticated, shorter-tail-finned B-52G and B-52H models for continued updating to spearhead the nuclear strike force. The B-52Ds were recalled to undergo a $30.6-million modification program called Big Belly, which would increase their bomb bay capacity from twenty-seven to eighty-four of the 500-pound conventional or "iron" bombs, with provision for another twenty-four on underwing pylons. This increased the bomb-carrying capacity of the B-52D to 54,000 pounds, over a capacity of 13,500 for the B-52F. On September 13, 1967, the Big Belly program was complete, and the B-52Ds were gradually replacing B-52Fs in the war zone. The latter were retired and put into mothballs.

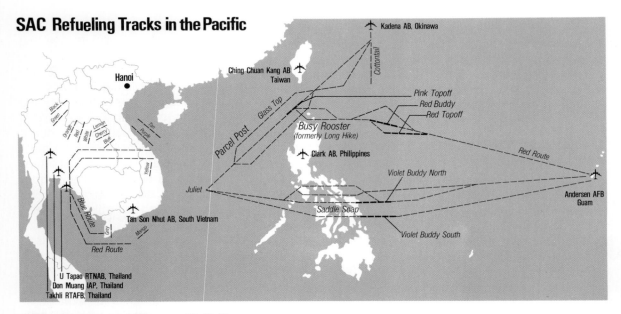

15 Expanding SAC Tanker Operations

Because of the distances involved in the Arc Light missions from Andersen AFB on Guam, the big bombers depended to a great extent on the SAC 4252d SW Young Tiger tankers operating out of Kadena. A year of supporting the Rolling Thunder tactical air operations out of Thailand and South Vietnam had given the tankers a chance to refine their procedures. After handling the F–105 "Thud" fighter-bombers that couldn't take on fuel above 16,000 to 17,000 feet (some had to be refueled as low as 5,000 feet), the B–52 refueling at the more routine 27,000 to 30,000 feet went somewhat more smoothly. To facilitate the Arc Light refueling, elaborate refueling tracks had to be established in the skies over the western Pacific. This requirement had been underscored by the collision between two

bombers on the first Arc Light mission back in June of 1965. As established, there would be a distance of 200 nautical miles between tracks, with 500 feet of altitude between bombers using the same track. The tracks were set up in the area of the Philippines about two thirds of the way from Andersen to the target area. The location of the tracks took into account the commercial traffic coming in and out of the Philippines and Taiwan.

The primary refueling track, Glass Top, was off the northwest coast of the main Philippine island of Luzon. The later Haybailer I and II refuelings used the same area as Glass Top, but with varied angles of approach. The alternate to Glass Top track was Busy Rooster in the area previously known as Long Hike, off the northeast coast of Luzon. The secondary refueling area lay across the central Philippines and was called Saddle Soap, with shortened or angled versions of Saddle Soap known as Spring High I and II. In addition there were tertiary tracks called top-

off routes. There were usually the same number of tankers as bombers, but a procedure that came to be called Odd Ball was developed so that two tankers could refuel a typical three-plane B–52 cell if one of the tankers had to abort.

On the return from a mission the bombers were a good deal lighter, having expended the weight of fuel and ordnance, and could usually make it home. However, in case poststrike refueling was required, Jumping Jack (later Constant Guard) tankers were on alert at Clark AB in the Philippines, and emergency strip alert tankers were on station back at Andersen.

Although the Kadena-based Young Tiger tankers were ideal for Arc Light operations originating at Guam, the smaller number of Tiger Cub tankers staging out of Don Muang were becoming overwhelmed by the work load required to

support tactical operations in South Vietnam. As early as July 1965, PACAF and SAC had recognized the need to base more tankers in Southeast Asia. An increase in operations from Don Muang was ruled out for political reasons (Don Muang was Bangkok International Airport); Korat and Takhli were initially ruled out because of the increased fighter activity there and concern that the runways couldn't stand up to sustained use by the heavier tankers; bases in South Vietnam were out because of the high level of tactical air activity and because none of the bases were really secure from Vietcong sapper attacks.

Ultimately, it was decided to base a limited

number of tankers at Takhli under the code name King Cobra. Takhli was chosen because it was closer to North Vietnam, Laos, and northern South Vietnam and because it could be used at night (unlike Don Muang, where night tanker operations were restricted, and some other bases that had no runway lights). By the beginning of 1966, there were forty-one tankers based at Kadena (thirty earmarked for Arc Light support and the rest for PACAF Southeast Asia operations), four at Don Muang, and ten King Cobras at Takhli.

At the same time the go-ahead had been given for construction of an all-new air base at Sattahip, Thailand. On August 11, 1966, the new base, now named U Tapao Royal Thai Navy Air Base, was opened for business with fifteen tankers forming the 4258th Strategic Wing. The operations from U Tapao came to be known by the code name Giant Cobra, partly because of the large number of these snakes inhabiting the base and surrounding areas. U Tapao became the main tanker base in Southeast Asia, with Takhli becoming a forward staging base as operations at Don Muang were phased out.

Throughout the next six months, as the war escalated and Arc Light and PACAF tactical operations increased, considerable thought was given to using U Tapao as an additional B–52 base and developing Kung Kuan (later Ching Chuan Kang) Nationalist Chinese Air Base on Taiwan as a tanker and/or bomber base. Eventually Ching Chuan Kang AB was used as a KC–135 base, but not until February 1968, after enormous engineering difficulties with the pipeline system at the base were overcome. When B–52 operations began from U Tapao on April 11, 1967, it was a boon to the tanker force because the B–52s no longer needed refueling as they had out of Andersen, and this freed a number of Kadena-based tankers to support PACAF operations.

During May 1967, SAC's KC–135s flew two of the most outstanding missions of their wartime careers. On May 3 a pair of F–105 Thunderchiefs were returning from a Rolling Thunder mission in North Vietnam. On the return the "Thuds" had burned up a good deal of fuel flying cover for a pilot who had been shot down. Both planes were in trouble. Their gas gauges were on *E,* and they were out of range of their base. The pilots got on the air to request an emergency refueling. So many Good Samaritans jumped on the frequency with offers of assistance that it was jammed with screeching static. Maj. Alvin Lewis, piloting a KC–135 in an adjoining track, did not respond verbally, because of the clutter. Instead, he broke off and made his way directly to their reported position, arriving just as one of the Thuds was going into a 20-degree dive and about to flame out. Lewis made contact with the Thud pilot just as he was ready to eject and maneuvered the huge tanker ahead of the diving fighter-bomber. By the time he had become linked to the KC–135's refueling boom, the Thud had flamed out from complete lack of fuel. Lewis now found himself in a 30-degree dive linked to a plane with a dead engine. With the murky Laotian jungle rushing up at them, fuel began to flow, and the Thud pilot finally got the engine restarted. The planes separated, pulled out of the dive, and Lewis proceeded to rescue the other plane. The net gain was two pilots and nearly five million dollars worth of airplanes.

On the last day of May, Maj. John Casteel and his KC–135 crew were over the Gulf of Tonkin on a routine mission when they were notified to contact the Navy's Task Force 77 about a possible emergency. Casteel was in the process of gassing up a pair of PACAF F–104s when he got the call, so he took them along, transferring fuel en route. As it turned out, two Navy A–3s from the aircraft carrier USS *Hancock,* tankers

themselves, were in trouble. One of the A–3s was down to three minutes of fuel. Though he had plenty of fuel in his transfer tanks, he couldn't transfer it into his own tanks. Casteel quickly transferred 2,300 pounds of fuel to the first A–3 and started on the second. Just then a pair of Navy F–8 fighters from the carrier USS *Bon-*

Above: A B-52D drops its bomb load on a target far below (see photos on pages 98 and 99).

homme Richard arrived on the scene. One of the planes was almost completely dry and needed to be refueled immediately, so he attached himself to the A–3 that was attached to the KC–

135. Charles Hopkins, in the official history of Southeast Asia refueling operations, cited it as the "first and probably only, three-deep refueling ever made." As fuel from the KC–135 was running through one plane and into another, the first A–3 began refueling the second F–8. Gradually the first A–3 began to run dry, and the KC–135 broke off from one pair of Navy planes and moved to the other. The KC–135 had now passed fuel to both A–3s at the same time they were themselves refueling F–8s.

By this time, the two F–104s that had accompanied the KC–135 were running low and needed to be refueled. Casteel had just transferred another 3000 pounds to each of them when a pair of Navy F–4s returning to the USS *Constellation,* desperately short of fuel, were vectored to the KC–135 for an emergency fill-up. The F–4s were refueled and then the F–104s for a third time. By this point the KC–135 was running low itself, and Casteel diverted the tanker to an alternate landing at Da Nang in South Vietnam. They arrived at Da Nang with 10,000 pounds of fuel, having transferred 49,000 pounds to eight aircraft in fourteen refuelings. For their efforts the tanker crewmen were awarded the McKay Trophy for the most meritorious flight of the year, the ninth SAC crew to receive the award.

16 Arc Light Rolls On

With the basing of B–52s at U Tapao, the Arc Light operations became smoother and more efficient. Not only did the Thailand-based bombers need no refueling, the mission time was cut from an average of twelve hours for Guam-based missions to an average of three hours from U Tapao. The crews could fly more sorties and get more rest. Ironically, because of the shorter mission times, the new scenario enhanced the ability of the big bombers to fly tactical or ground-support missions. The big strategic bombers had been in the war for two years and had yet to fly a strategic bombing mission.

The Rolling Thunder missions "up North" were being flown by tactical aircraft, principally F–105 fighter-bombers with F–4s along as fighter escorts (MiG Combat Air Patrol or MiG CAP). Because of the Johnson administration's reluctance to utilize any kind of strategic airpower for fear of hitting civilians, most of the F–105/F–4 Rolling Thunder missions were tactical. It was a topsy-turvy application of airpower, in which carpet bombing of hundreds of acres of South Vietnamese jungle was preferable to interdicting the same enemy weapons by destroying a twenty-foot-wide bridge in North Vietnam. The North Vietnamese didn't take long to realize that a great number of the juiciest strategic targets were safe from attack. Their capital city of Hanoi, with its important railheads and factories, and the port city of Haiphong were generally off-limits. Surface-to-air missile (SAM) batteries located in residential areas were generally safe as well. When the North Vietnamese learned that their fragile system of dikes that protected vast areas of farmland and residential areas from disastrous flooding were safe from attack, they taunted the Americans by placing SAM batteries on the dikes. If an American plane returned the fire from such a site, he would destroy the dike, and the world press would be told about the barbaric Americans, who flooded farms.

Despite the general ban on strategic bombing, an occasional strategic target would get approval from the command authorities in Washington. One example was petroleum and lubricant facilities near both Hanoi and Haiphong that were struck on June 29, 1966, by PACAF fighter-bombers, with excellent results. Another was the March 10, 1967, PACAF raid on the Thai Nguyen iron and steel works near Hanoi. North Vietnam was actually among the world's important steel producers, and Thai Nguyen was North Vietnam's largest steel mill and the only one in all of Southeast Asia with the capacity to produce bridge sections, barges, and oil drums. It was one of the most important strategic targets in North Vietnam and had remained off the approved Rolling Thunder target list for two years.

As Rolling Thunder rolled north, Arc Light continued, mostly in South Vietnam. Among the reasons for restricting the B–52s to missions in the South was self-preservation. North Vietnam desperately wanted to shoot down a B–52. To be able to show the world that tiny North Vietnam had shot down America's first-line strategic bomber would be a tremendous propaganda coup. In South Vietnam B–52s were safe from hostile fire at the altitudes they flew, whereas the North bristled with SAMs and MiGs. On September 17, 1967, the North Vietnamese got their first chance at a B–52. SAMs had been moved into the southernmost part of North Vietnam, where B–52s sometimes operated. A three-plane cell came into range and two SAMs streaked aloft, but the big bombers took evasive action and there was no kill. Though they made two more attempts during 1967 to down a B–52, it would be another five years before enemy action would inflict a mortal wound.

Early 1968 saw several major changes in the course of the war. First came the North Vietnamese Tet (Lunar New Year) Offensive in January. Using large numbers of troops, including conventional forces rather than guerrillas, they put American and South Vietnamese forces on the defensive throughout South Vietnam, even penetrating the American embassy building in Saigon. The Americans and their allies prevailed in the end, but it was a tough fight, a serious psychological blow.

Another psychological turning point came on the heels of Tet with the New Hampshire Democratic presidential primary. The primary pitted President Johnson against antiwar Senator Eugene McCarthy, who was riding an ever-rising tide of antiwar sentiment. Though Johnson won, McCarthy made a strong showing, strong enough, in fact, to cause Johnson to opt not to continue the race for re-election. Johnson perceived that the American electorate wanted an end to the war, and he decided to adopt a course of gradual withdrawal of American forces combined with an attempt at a negotiated settlement.

In his televised address on March 31, 1968, Johnson told the nation: "I am taking the first step to de-escalate the conflict. Tonight I have ordered our aircraft and naval vessels to make no attacks on North Vietnam except in the area north of the demilitarized zone . . . our purpose in this action is to bring about a reduction in the level of violence that exists."

As the 1968 election campaign progressed, Johnson's vice president, Hubert Humphrey, was nominated as the Democractic presidential candidate; the Republicans nominated Richard Nixon, who took the lead in the opinion polls. On November 1, with the election four days away, in a move aimed partly at helping Humphrey win and partly at responding to alleged understandings with North Vietnamese negotiators, Johnson called a complete halt to *all* bombing missions in North Vietnam. Humphrey lost, Nixon won, the bombing halt stayed in place, and the war continued unabated in the South.

U.S. airpower was now diverted to Commando Hunt operations, the continued attempts to stop the flow of matériel to the South by bombing the Ho Chi Minh Trail in Laos, and to ground support in South Vietnam. Although the attack sorties over North Vietnam were curtailed, reconnaissance sorties were not. What these flights discovered was that the North Viet-

namese, far from winding down their activities, were frantically building up their damaged logistical system, which had suffered four years of bombing, in order to support wider and more sustained offensive activities.

A change in attitude could now be seen among America's airmen in Vietnam: there was coming to be widespread support for the type of strategic bombing offensive that General LeMay had proposed four years earlier. The official PACAF history of the period states:

Commando Hunt interdiction campaigns, although impressive in scope and effective in reducing the flow of supplies to enemy forces in South Vietnam and exacting a painful price from the enemy, were limited in overall effectiveness by the nature of the targets. A more effective campaign would have directed maximum effort against the North's vital supply targets such as factories, power plants, refineries, marshaling yards, and bulk transportation lines. National policies placed these lucrative targets off-limits,

and the alternative was to wait until the supplies had been disseminated among thousands of trucks, sampans, rafts, and bicycles, which made the tasks of detecting and destroying them nearly impossibly difficult. Commando Hunt required that valuable, multi-million-dollar aircraft be sent after individual vehicles and similar low-value targets, in the face of increasingly effective antiaircraft defenses. This tactic not only failed to halt the flow of supplies but also maximized costs to the U.S. rather than the enemy.

A House Armed Services Committee report stated that, since the 1 November 1968 bombing halt, the enormous increase in North Vietnamese logistics operations toward Laos and the DMZ were of such volume that it appeared that they were establishing a massive logistics system as a foundation for future expanded operations. The report concluded that if the peace talks failed, the bombing halt will have provided the North with a new lease on life, and the war would drag on.

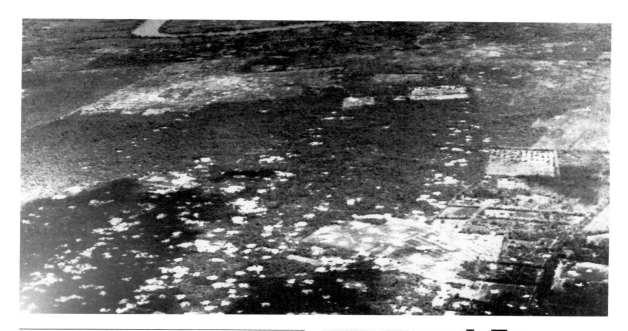

Left: The bombs of an Arc Light B-52 carve a swath across the South Vietnamese jungle.
Above and right: The aftermath of Arc Light; rows of bomb craters and jungles turned to deserts of burnt match sticks.

As the stalemate continued, Arc Light sorties dropped from 1,800 to 1,600 per month in July 1969, and to a rate of 1,400 in October. For the year, however, the number of Arc Light sorties (19,498) was down only slightly from the 1968 peak of 20,568, and was still more than double the 1967 total of 9,686. During 1970, Arc Light missions, even though they had expanded to Laos and Cambodia, were down to 15,103; and the next year, as the war was being seen to de-escalate, the number dropped further, to 12,552.

In 1970, SAC's illustrious Eighth Air Force entered the Vietnam War though its participation was to be short-lived. With the reduction of conventional SAC forces underway back in the States, it had been decided to deactivate the Eighth, which would leave SAC with only two numbered air forces (the Second and the Fifteenth) for the first time since 1949 when the second was reassigned. At the last minute, largely because of the World War II heritage of the Eighth—the most famous of all the USAF numbered air forces—the decision was reversed. Eighth Air Force headquarters at Westover AFB, Massachusetts, was closed as planned on March 31, 1970, but on the same day it was reactivated at Andersen AFB on Guam, assuming the personnel and mission of the 3d Air Division. The Eighth Air Force was now flying combat missions in its third war. It lasted only a few months, however, as on September 19, all B−52 operations from Guam were eliminated in favor of the shorter distance between U Tapao and the targets. The bombers at Andersen reverted to their prewar status, that of being on alert for retaliation in case of nuclear attack. Also during that September, B−52 operations from Kadena—which had been kept secret because of political unrest on Okinawa—were phased out.

17 "Press On"

On the night of March 29/30, 1972, forty-one months after Lyndon Johnson had imposed the bombing halt, North Vietnam abandoned its doctrine of infiltration and guerrilla warfare and launched a massive invasion of South Vietnam. They attacked with twelve divisions of regular troops supported by tanks and artillery. What had been regarded as a guerrilla insurrection or a civil war, turned overnight into a full-scale conventional war. Previous rules of engagement went out the window, and with them, the bombing halt.

The Tactical Air Command quickly deployed a large number of F−105Gs and F−4Es from bases in the States to Korat and Ubon air bases in Thailand. SAC sent the B−52s north on April 9. Two days later, the B−52s struck Vinh, and on the fifteenth they attacked petroleum and lubricant storage dumps near Haiphong.

On May 8 President Richard Nixon announced an air offensive, code-named Linebacker, against North Vietnam. Rail lines in the heart of North Vietnam would be bombed, and—eight years after it was first proposed by Curtis LeMay—North Vietnamese ports would be mined to "keep the weapons of war out of the hands of the international outlaws" in Hanoi.

By June SAC had assembled for their Arc Light operations a force of 206 B−52s, the largest number ever deployed at one time in the war. The Arc Light strikes were now being flown from U Tapao and, for the first time since 1970, Guam as well. By this time there were 172 KC−135s flying out of U Tapao and Kadena. It was the largest tanker fleet ever assembled.

The year 1972 was, like 1968, an election year, and escalating a war during an election year is, for a president, like passing a tax hike would be for a legislative body. Thus, though election victory was much more certain for Nixon in 1972 than for Humphrey in 1968, there came a bombing halt north of the 20th parallel. On October 23, 1972, Linebacker, the most intensive air offensive that North Vietnam had yet endured, drew to a close. It had been announced that an agreement was at hand in the Paris peace talks. In fact, Le Duc Tho, North Vietnam's obstinate little chief negotiator, was as intransigent as ever, and peace was not at hand. North Vietnam simply wanted to lure the Americans into a bombing halt so that they could lick their Linebacker-singed wounds. The election came, Richard Nixon was re-elected, and the B−52s continued flying from both U Tapao and Andersen to targets below the 20th parallel.

As the election receded into memory, the war began to crank up once more. It was 1968 all over again: a couple of weeks after the bombing halt, the North Vietnamese began to intensify their offensive. This time the B–52 crews echoed the Curtis LeMay of eight years before. There was strong sentiment for stopping the enemy then and there. Despite strain on men and machine alike, the order of the day, heretofore rarely heard, came in two words: "press on."

In the past four years, North Vietnam had erected the world's most intense air defense system. This included not only a porcupine's back of SAMs and antiaircraft guns around Hanoi but SAMs throughout the southern part of North Vietnam as well. They had yet to claim a B–52, but not for want of trying.

The city of Vinh, the most important railhead in the southern part of the country, bristled with SAMs. It was into this hellhole that many of November's Arc Light missions were targeted. On the night of the twenty-second, Capt. N. J. Ostrozny's B–52D out of U Tapao was flying the number two position in Olive Cell into Vinh. Moments after "bombs away," a tremendous explosion ripped the belly of the big bomber. Fires erupted in both wings. Communication lines were ripped out.

It didn't take the crew long to decide what to do. As long as the plane had forward velocity, there would be no parachutes. Nobody inside felt like checking into a North Vietnamese prison camp for an interminable future of cold rice and abuse. Ostrozny tried to keep the huge burning shard aloft and on course for Thailand, while Sgt. Ron Sellers, the gunner, his intercom dead, sat in his tail turret watching the number 7 and 8 engines turning into a ball of fire. Sellers watched as the skin burned off the starboard wing. One by one the damaged engines flamed out. First four, then six. Five miles from the Mekong River, the Thai border, and safety, the last engine was gone. The starboard wing tip dropped away in a whirling cloud of sparks, and two hundred tons of B–52 started to bank uncontrollably. There was now no electricity in the plane except for the bail-

out lights. It was time. Navigator Capt. Bob Estes confirmed they were in Thailand, and the crew left the huge, burning coffin. They bailed out near Nakhon Phanom AB and were promptly recovered and returned to U Tapao. But the North Vietnamese had claimed their first B–52.

18 Linebacker II

Even before Ostrozny's B–52 slammed into a Thai mountainside, even before Nixon's October 20 bombing halt, something big was in the works at Eighth Air Force headquarters out on Guam. Bullet Shot was the code name for the operation that had brought over one hundred fifty B–52s to the island. Not only were B–52Ds being flown in, but nearly one hundred of the more sophisticated B–52Gs as well. Under normal conditions Andersen could accommodate around three thousand personnel, but that number had gone up to four thousand supporting the Arc Light operations that had mushroomed over the summer. Now Bullet Shot had caused the population of the base to swell to over twelve thousand. The quarters were overflowing. Tent cities and unair-conditioned tin buildings proliferated all over the island.

On December 16, 1972, there was a meeting at Eighth Air Force headquarters. Lt. Col. Hendsley Conner, commanding the 486th Bomb Squadron, remembers the meeting:

Everyone was still hopeful that a truce would be reached in time for us to "get home in time for Christmas." All but a few bombing missions had been canceled for December seventeenth. A meeting for all commanders was scheduled for 1400 on the sixteenth in the Eighth Air Force commander's conference room. What was in the air? Were they getting the airplanes ready for us to fly home?

As we gathered for the meeting, speculation

was running about fifty-fifty that we would be going home. Others of us had a premonition and were saying nothing. The general came in, and the meeting got under way. The briefing officer opened the curtain over the briefing board and there it was—we were not going home. Not yet, anyway. We were going North. Our targets were to be Hanoi and Haiphong, North Vietnam. At last the B–52 bomber force would be used in the role it had been designed for. The goal of this new operation was to attempt to destroy the war-making capability of the enemy.

The method of attack we were to use would be night, high-altitude, radar bombing of all military targets in the area of the two major cities in North Vietnam. We would launch a raid each night beginning on the eighteenth of December and continue with a raid each night. Each raid would consist of three waves of varying strength, each hitting their targets at four- to five-hour intervals.

It would not be easy. We would suffer losses. The Hanoi/Haiphong target complex was among the most heavily defended areas in the world. The combined number of surface-to-air missiles, fighter aircraft, and antiaircraft guns that surrounded the target area exceeded anything ever experienced.

It would be called Linebacker II. Scheduled to continue for three nights of "maximum effort," this would be the first strategic air offensive since Korea, and the first of its kind since 1945. It would star the grandson of the Boeing B–17 Flying Fortress, son of the Boeing B–29 Superfortress—the Boeing B–52 Stratofortress. These three planes would come to epitomize the American strategic bomber, and the third generation of Boeing's "forts" would carve out an important niche in the history of strategic bombing. Called Stratofortress by its manufacturer, during the war in Southeast Asia, the B–52 came to be known by its crews simply as BUFF, one of those nick-

names of self-deprecating endearment that comes along from time to time with certain airplanes. In the lexicon of the crews that have come to know and love them the F–105 Thunderchief is known universally as "Thud," the F–111 as "Aardvark," and the UH–1 Iroquois helicopter as "Huey," and today the A–10 Thunderbolt is called "Warthog." The name BUFF had less to do with the plane's camouflage color (applied in the war zone to the once-silver B–52s) than with the acronym for its longer, less-repeatable nickname "Big Ugly Fat Fucker."

December 18, the opening night of Linebacker II, would see eighty-seven bombers fly from Andersen, fifty-four of them B–52Gs. They would be preceded by forty-two B–52Ds from U Tapao, assigned to smash the MiG bases at Kep, Hoa Loc, and—the big base—Phuc Yen. One hundred twenty-nine bombers would head to the target the first night, with nearly a hundred scheduled for each of the next two. At Andersen it would be an air controller's nightmare. The round-trip flight-time to the targets was around fourteen hours, meaning that the second night's attackers would be taking off as the first night's bombers returned, some undoubtedly with battle damage. Some bombers would be in need of emergency refueling from the strip tankers, who would have to take off amid the bombers being launched.

The logistical support would be strained beyond belief. Normally, the Arc Light missions required six crew buses. For Linebacker II, a dozen times that many, or more, would have to be scrounged. The mess would have to pack five hundred box lunches at a time instead of a leisurely two dozen every three hours.

Tactics had to be designed for the big bombers, flying en masse into a MiG-and-SAM-intense environment for the first time. The attackers would carry electronic countermeasures (ECM) packages like the fighter-bombers carried when going to "downtown Hanoi." The ECM packs countered the electronic guidance systems used to route the SAMs to their targets. The ECM equipment was designed so that its effectiveness was compounded when integrated within a three-plane cell. The image of the planes on enemy radar and on SAM target-tracking radar would become jammed with static. Should one of the three planes fall out of cell formation, the shielding effect of the integrated ECM of the cell would be shattered, and the planes would come sharply into focus, suddenly at the mercy of the SAMs. For this reason, and to avoid collisions in the dark, crowded air space, SAC ordered the B–52s to stay together. They were not to break formation even to take evasive action to avoid a SAM.

The morning of December 18, 1972, was hot and clear on Guam. There had been routine Arc Light sorties flown on the seventeenth, but everyone knew today would be different. Until the morning briefing only the commanders knew the whole story. Col. (later General) James R. McCarthy, commander of the 43d Strategic Wing and one of the key planners of Linebacker II, recalled:

As the crews filed into the briefing room there was the usual milling around and small talk between crew members, made the more so by the large numbers of people.

Since I was selected to give all three briefings on the first day, I tried to come up with some words or phrases that would convey the message of the importance of the targets to our national goals, yet I wanted to keep it simple and uncluttered. After a few minutes' debate with myself I chose the simplest of opening statements. As the route was shown on the briefing screen I said, "Gentlemen, your target for tonight is Hanoi." It must have been effective, because for the rest of the briefing you could have heard a pin drop.

At a few minutes before three on the afternoon of the eighteenth, Maj. Bill Stocker's B–52D began the takeoff roll down Andersen's swaybacked runway. Ninety seconds after Stocker's plane lurched into the air, it was followed by another, then another.

Lt. Col. George Allison, one of the pilots who had flown to South Vietnam with Arc Light the day before, was watching. He recalled later:

It was difficult to describe a feeling which develops gradually around intuition, hunches, rumors, logic, and so forth, but subsequently draws its substance from fact. Was it happiness, relief, a sense of "we're finally going to do it; it's long overdue"? Or was it dismay, confusion, a sense of "has it actually come to this"? I can't remember, and I'm satisfied that I can't because all of these feelings were intermingled in the fascination of the moment.

Ever so slowly, the reality and significance started to sink in. As the first of the flight crews prepared for launch, clusters of people started to gather here and there. Many took advantage of the balconies on the multistoried crew billets to watch the scene unfold. It was an occasion for conversation, poor jokes, more rumors, and sober reflection. Somebody out there wasn't going to come back, and we all knew it. The vantage point from the crew quarters lent itself to the drama of the occasion. The runway was plainly visible, and each launch could be watched up through a point at which the crew was positively committed to a takeoff. That point of commitment, essential to every takeoff, took on special meaning as we watched.

The most impressive sight, however, was the preliminary to the launch. For, from this same vantage point, the only portion of most of the taxiing force which was visible was the vertical stabilizers. They could be seen moving along the line of revetments, an assembly line of aircraft tails. The similarity of these to the moving tar-

gets in a shooting gallery stuck in my mind. I didn't like the analogy, but it was too vivid to dismiss. They would move forward, ever so slowly, but the line seemed to never stop. A constant procession of aircraft tails, almost too much to grasp. Where were they all coming from to get in a continuous line like that? When would the line end? We don't have that many B–52s on the whole island!—which can be the sensation when you've lost count.

Finally around midnight they were all airborne, and the ensuing silence was as thunderous as the hours of launches. It was time to grab a bite to eat, do a lot of thinking, and take a quick glance at the next day's list of fliers. Probably wouldn't be anything going after an effort like this, but checking was part of the required routine. That was a bad guess on my part, and the next day it would be my turn.

Wave II had begun the takeoff roll at about seven in the evening. Lt. Col. Hendsley Conner, who had been at the initial briefing on the sixteenth, was now Airborne Mission Commander and a passenger in the number 2 of Peach Cell in Wave II. After the awesome takeoff it was a routine flight. Conner slept for about three hours until the planes slipped into the refueling track.

Even as Wave II from Andersen was lifting off, the first wave of B–52Ds out of U Tapao were making their turn at the Initial Point near Dai Thi about a hundred nautical miles north-northwest of Hanoi. It was 7:43 P.M. local time at Hao Loc Air Base fifteen miles from downtown Hanoi when the first string of 750-pounders from Snow 1 thundered into the runway and hangar complex.

Fifteen hundred miles away in the gathering dusk, Peach 2 was exiting the refueling with its tanks topped off.

Conners tuned in the radio to hear how the lead wave was doing.

The first report I heard was when Colonel Rew made his call-in after they exited the target area. They had had a tough experience. One airplane was known to be shot down by SAMs, two were presently not accounted for, and one had received heavy battle damage. He initially estimated that the North Vietnamese had fired over two hundred SAMs at them. There were no reports of MiG fighter attacks. The antiaircraft artillery was heavy, but well below their flight level. For us, the worst part was now they knew we were coming, and things probably would be even worse when we got there.

I saw the SAMs as we came in closer to the target area. They made white streaks of light as they climbed into the night sky. As they left the ground, they would move slowly, pick up speed as they climbed, and end their flight, finally, in a cascade of sparkles. There were so many of them it reminded me of a Fourth of July fireworks display. A beautiful sight to watch if I hadn't known how lethal they could be. I had flown over two hundred missions in B–57s and I thought I knew what was in store for us, but I had never seen so many SAMs. I did not feel nearly as secure in the big lumbering bomber as I had in my B–57 Canberra that could maneuver so much better.

Just before we started our bomb run, we checked our emergency gear to make sure everything was all right in case we were hit. We would be most vulnerable on the bomb run, since we would be within lethal range of the SAMs and would be flying straight and level. We had been briefed not to make any evasive maneuvers on the bomb run so that the radar navigator would be positive he was aiming at the right target. If he was not absolutely sure he had the right target, we were to withhold our bombs and then jettison them into the ocean on our way back to Guam. We did not want to hit anything but military targets. Precision bombing was the object of our mission. The crews were briefed this way and they followed their instructions.

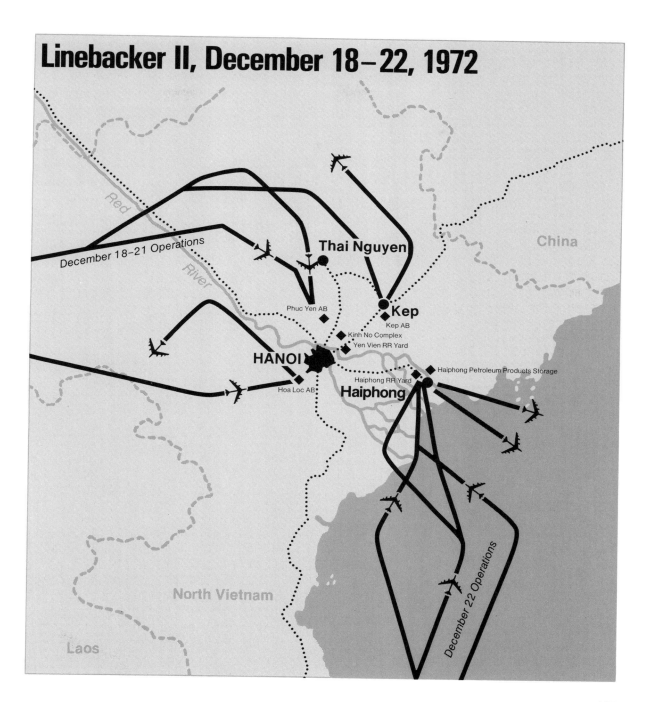

Linebacker II, December 18–22, 1972

December 18–21 Operations

Thai Nguyen

Phuc Yen AB

Kep
Kep AB

Kinh No Complex
Yen Vien RR Yard

HANOI

Hoa Loc AB

Haiphong RR Yard
Haiphong

Haiphong Petroleum Products Storage

December 22 Operations

North Vietnam

Laos

China

Red
River

About halfway down the bomb run, the electronic warfare officer on our crew began to call over the interphone that SAMs had been fired at us. One, two, three, now four, missiles had been fired. We flew straight and level.

"How far out from the target are we, Radar?"

"We're ten seconds out. Five. Four. Three. Two. One. BOMBS AWAY! Start your . . . turn, pilot."

We began a . . . right turn to exit the target area.

KABOOM! We were hit.

It felt like we had been in the center of a clap of thunder. The noise was deafening. Everything went really bright for an instant, then dark again. I could smell ozone from burnt powder, and had felt a slight jerk on my right shoulder.

I quickly checked the flight instruments and over the interphone said, "Pilot, we're still flying. Are you okay?"

"Yes, I'm fine, but the airplane is in bad shape. Let's check it over and see if we can keep it airborne. . . ."

I called the lead aircraft to let them know we had been hit. He said he could tell we had been hit because our left wing was on fire and we were slowing down. I asked him to call some escort fighters for us.

The airplane continued to fly all right, so the pilot resumed making evasive maneuvers. We flew out of the range of the missiles, finally, and began to take stock of the airplane.

The SAM had exploded right off our left wing. The fuel tank on that wing was missing along with part of the wingtip. We had lost number 1 and number 2 engines. Fire was streaming out of the wreckage they had left. Fuel was coming out of holes all throughout the left wing. Most of our flight instruments were not working. We had lost cabin pressurization. We were at 30,000 feet altitude. Our oxygen supply must have been hit, because the quantity gauge was slowly decreasing. I took out two walkaround bottles for the pilot and copilot. If we ran out, they, at least, would have enough emergency oxygen to get us down to an altitude where we could breathe.

We turned to a heading that would take us to U Tapao, Thailand. . . .

Two F–4s had joined us and would stay with us as long as they were needed. One stayed high, and the other stayed on our wing, as we descended to a lower altitude and to oxygen. They called to alert rescue service in case we had to abandon the aircraft. Our first concern was to get out of North Vietnam and Laos. We did not want to end up as POWs. We knew they did not take many prisoners in Laos.

Thailand looked beautiful when we finally crossed the border. Since Thailand was not subject to bombing attacks, they still had their lights on at night. We flew for about thirty minutes after we had descended to a lower altitude, and began to think we would be able to get the airplane on the ground safely. . . .

I unfastened my lap belt and leaned over between the pilot and copilot to take another look at the fire. It had now spread to the fuel leaking out of the wing, and the whole left wing was burning. It was a wall of red flame starting just outside the cockpit and as high as I could see. . . .

The six crewmembers in the B–52G have ejection seats that they fire to abandon the aircraft. Anyone else on board has to go down to the lower compartment and manually bail out of the hole the navigator or radar navigator leaves when their seat is ejected. I quickly climbed down the ladder and started to plug in my interphone cord to see what our situation was.

The red ABANDON light came on.

BAM! The navigator fired his ejection seat and was gone.

The Radar turned toward me and pointed to

the hole the navigator had left and motioned for me to jump. I climbed over some debris and stood on the edge of the hole. I looked at the ground far below. Did I want to jump? The airplane began to shudder and shake, and I heard other explosions as the other crewmembers ejected. I heard another louder blast. The wing was exploding. Yes, I wanted to jump! I rolled through the opening, and as soon as I thought I was free of the airplane, I pulled the ripcord on my parachute. . . .

There was a full moon, the weather was clear, and I could see things very well. I looked for other parachutes. One, two, three; that's all I saw. Then I saw the airplane. It was flying in a descending turn to the left; the whole fuselage was now burning, and parts of the left wing had left the airplane. It was exploding as it hit the ground.

I saw I was getting close to the ground, so I got ready to land. I was floating backwards, but I could see I was going to land in a little village. I raised my legs to keep from going into a hootch. I certainly didn't want to land in someone's bedroom. I got my feet down, hit the ground, and rolled over on my backside. . . . It felt good to be alive.

The plan for the second night of Linebacker II would replicate the December 18 missions. The approach would be the same: out of the northwest into downtown Hanoi with the Kinh No railroad and storage complex on the top of the target list for Wave I. Waves II and III would hit the Yen Vien railroad complex, and Wave III would also attack the Thai Nguyen thermal power plant. Colonel McCarthy, in the lead B–52 of White Cell recalled that just as the bombers made their turn at the Initial Point his electronic warfare officer, responsible for detecting and assessing the SAM threat, picked up the homing radar of the first SAMs locking onto White 1.

Suddenly, the gunner broke in on interphone to report that he had two SAMs, low, heading right for us. The EW confirmed that they were tracking toward us. The copilot then reported four missiles coming our way on the right side. Added to the pyrotechnics were Shrike antiradiation missile firings, which would give us momentary concern until we identified them. Then it was nice to watch something bright streaking the other way—our guys had their own bag of tricks. The pilot then reported two missiles coming up on his side. The nav team downstairs was busy trying to complete their checklist for the bomb run. Other aircraft and Red Crown were also calling SAM warnings and antiaircraft fire. The primary radio frequency quickly became saturated. As we approached Hanoi, we could see other SAMs being fired. As one was fired on the ground, an area about the size of a city block would be lit up by the flash. It looked as if a whole city block had suddenly caught fire. This area was magnified by the light cloud undercast over Hanoi at the time. As the missile broke through the clouds, the large lighted area was replaced by a ring of silver fire that appeared to be the size of a basketball. This was the exhaust of the rocket motor that would grow brighter as the missile approached the aircraft. The rocket exhaust of a missile that was fired at you from the front quarter would take on the appearance of a lighter silver doughnut. Some crews nicknamed them the "deadly doughnuts."

At about 120 seconds prior to bombs away, the SAMs were replaced by AAA fire. There were two types. Of most concern were the large, ugly black explosions that came from the big 100mm guns. Then there would be smaller multicolored flak at lower altitudes, almost a pleasure to watch by contrast. There would be a silver-colored explosion, followed by several orange explosions clustered around the first silver burst. About 60 seconds before bombs away, the flak was again replaced by SAMs. This time there were more of them and they exploded closer to the aircraft.

There was no doubt about it—they were getting our range.

About this time there was a call from a cell back in the wave reporting MiGs and requesting MiG CAP. At one minute prior to bombs away, the EW's scope became saturated with strong SAM lock-on signals. It was also at this point in the run that the bomb bay doors were opened. There had been, and would continue to be, quite a bit of discussion by the staff and crews as to whether opening of the bomb doors, exposing the mass of bombs to reflect radar energy to the SAM sites, gave the enemy an even brighter target to shoot at.

About ten seconds prior to bombs away, when the EW was reporting the strongest signals, we observed a Shrike being fired, low and forward of our nose. Five seconds later, several SAM signals dropped off the air, and the EW reported they were no longer a threat to our aircraft.

The BUFF began a slight shudder as the bombs left the racks. The aircraft, being relieved of nearly twenty-two tons of ordnance, wanted to raise rapidly, and it took a double handful of stick and throttles to keep it straight and level. After the release was complete and the bomb doors closed, Tom Lebar put the aircraft in a steep turn to the right. A second later, a SAM exploded where the right wing had been. The turn had saved us, but the gunner and copilot reported more SAMs on the way.

It seemed like the turn was going to last forever, and the copilot reported the SAMs tracking the aircraft and getting closer. It was now a race to see if we could complete the turn before the SAMs reached our altitude. Once the turn was completed we would be free to make small maneuvers, because the other aircraft in our cell would still be in the . . . turn.

It is strange what goes through your mind at a time like this. My thoughts were: "What the hell am I doing here?" With a lung full of what

eventually turned into double pneumonia and no ejection seat, I wasn't exactly an ideal insurance risk.

If SAC headquarters had been writing the policy, they probably wouldn't have agreed with McCarthy. Buoyed by the loss of no bombers the second night against three the first, SAC decided that it would be worth the risk to continue the same "out of the northwest" attack plan on the third night. It proved to be a dreadful mistake.

Even as the triumphant second-night crews were touching down at Andersen on December 20, the third night's mission was starting out. The operations had been running continuously for over forty-eight hours, and things were going smoothly as the big bombers rolled out over the Pacific toward the Glass Top refueling track and the last night of the three-day maximum effort.

What they were flying into, however, was the night "all hell broke loose." Hanoi, blessed by Soviet benefactors with a superb air defense system, forewarned, or guessing that it would be a three-day effort, used their defenses sparingly on night two, but would turn them on full blast for the last night. Over 220 SAMs would be fired at the three waves.

The first cells slipped through, as the North Vietnamese noted their direction and turning points. Then Quilt 3 going into the Yen Vien complex was caught in the fusillade and went down. Capt. John Ellinger's Brass 2 was hit in the post-target turn, but they made it to Thailand before they had to ditch. Maj. John Stewart's Orange 3 was in the final bomb run when a pair of SAMs turned the plane into a swirling, phosphorescent cloud of twisted metal.

Approaching the Initial Point turn northwest to Hanoi, Capt. Roland Scott remembered that the time, track, and target location were nearly the same as his mission on the eighteenth.

Shortly after takeoff, we lost one engine and flew the mission on seven. That wasn't too serious a problem in the G model, but I would have felt better if it hadn't happened.

On the southeast leg approaching the IP, my copilot stated he saw a MiG-21 on the right wing of our aircraft. In mild disbelief, I stretched to see out his window, and sure enough, a MiG-21 with lights off was flying tight formation with us. I believe we could actually see the pilot. The approach of the fighter had not been detected by onboard systems. Shortly, two or three minutes, the copilot reported the MiG had departed. Almost immediately I saw the same, or another, enemy aircraft flying formation on the left side of us. After less than a minute it departed.

Our sighs of relief were short-lived, and we quickly learned what the MiGs had been up to. We visually detected missiles approaching from our eleven and one o'clock positions. I was extremely worried that missiles were also approaching from our rear that we could not see. The EW reported no uplink or downlink signals with the missiles this mission as were reported on the night of the eighteenth. However, these missiles appeared to be a lot more accurate than on the eighteenth. They seemed to readjust their track as I made small turns. I waited for each to get as close as I dared, and then would make a hard, although relatively small, maneuver in hopes of avoiding them.

They arrived in pairs, just a few seconds apart. Some, as they passed, would explode—a few close enough to shake my aircraft. In fact, one exploded so close and caused such a loud noise and violent shock that I stated to the crew that I thought we had been hit. In a very few seconds, after assessing engine instruments and control responses, and having received an OK from downstairs, I determined we had not been hit, or were at least under normal control, and we continued the bomb run. Apparently the MiG-21 we saw was flying with us to report heading, altitude, and airspeed to the missile sites.

Scott and his crew were among the lucky, but as they completed the bomb run and drove south across Laos and the Thai border, they watched the fireball of Brass 2 going down (Brass 2 was a plane lost and a crew saved).

It was a sobering night for SAC Deputy Chief of Staff Brig. Gen. Harry Cordes and the rest of the staff watching the carnage back at SAC Headquarters. Six out of ninety-three of the bombers went down, for a 7 percent loss rate, the worst night of the campaign—and of the war—for SAC. General Cordes pointed out that the darkest hour was just as dark at SAC headquarters as it was at Guam and U Tapao.

In addition to the personal concern of the SAC staff, there was pressure from many external sources. Such expressions as "Stop the carnage!" "We can't lose any more B-52s!" "It's become a blood bath!" were commonplace. General Meyer, Commander in Chief, SAC, felt many pressures. Many people in Washington were worried that the Air Force would fail—that the U.S. couldn't bring Hanoi to its knees. Many senior Air Force people were concerned that if the bombing continued, we would lose too many bombers, and airpower doctrine would have proven fallacious. Or, if the bombing were stopped, the same thing would occur. Admiral Moorer, Chairman, JCS, was concerned, but left the ultimate decision to General Meyer.

General Meyer experienced first-hand the "loneliness of command." He and he alone must make the decision. He listened as a judge to all the evidence. He polled every single man in the room—general, colonel, captain, lieutenant—go or no-go? He polled Jerry Johnson—can the crews take it? Then he made his decision, probably the most difficult of his career: "PRESS ON!"

The three-day maximum effort now became an effort of indefinite duration. Most of the losses on the third night were from the half of the B-52G fleet without the intensified ECM packages carried by the rest of the B–52Gs. It was decided that Andersen, from which all the B–52Gs flew, would stand down for the next two nights and the missions be flown by thirty B–52Ds from U Tapao. Their shorter distance to Hanoi meant need for fuel could be traded for a heavier bomb load destined for Quang Te Air Base and storage facilities at Bac Mai and Van Dien.

It was another dark night. Scarlet Cell got separated over Bac Mai and lost its mutual ECM effect; two bombers connected with SAMs. Four minutes behind them, Lt. Col. Bill Conlee was leading Blue Cell toward a 3:47 A.M. release time. His copilot, Capt. Dave Drummond, said, "It looks like we'll walk on SAMs tonight" as he watched the missile activity ahead. Between the Initial Point and the bomb release point Conlee remembered ten SAMs were fired in the vicinity of Blue Cell.

At bombs away we were bracketed by two SAMs, one going off below us and to the left, the second exploding above us and to the right. Shrapnel cracked the pilot's outer window glass, started fires in the left wing, and wounded Lieutenant Colonel Yuill, the pilot; Lieutenant Colonel Bernasconi, the radar navigator; Lieutenant Mayall, the navigator; and myself. We also experienced a rapid decompression and loss of electrical power. Shortly after this, with the fire worsening, Lieutenant Colonel Yuill gave the emergency bail-out signal via the alarm light and I ejected from the aircraft.

During free-fall two more SAMs passed me, and I attempted to look for our aircraft, but was unable to see it. I was also unable to see any other chutes in the darkness. I realized after my chute had opened at preset altitude that my left arm was numb and that I had lost my glove from my left hand during ejection. I also realized that I was bleeding profusely from the face and arm due to shrapnel wounds. I deployed the survival kit with my right hand and prepared for landing.

I steered for an open field, just missing going into a large river, and believed that I would land undetected.

About two hundred to three hundred feet from touchdown, my illusions were shattered when small arms fire was directed at me. I ignored the firing and concentrated on making a good landing. I touched down, dumped my chute and took off my helmet, and at once was set upon by a mob of North Vietnamese, both civilian and military. They immediately took my gun, my watch, and my boots. They then stripped me at gunpoint to my underwear and forced me to run for approximately a mile through a gauntlet of people with farm implements, clubs, and bamboo poles. During this wild scene, several of their blows succeeded in breaking ribs and badly damaging my right knee. The mob scene ended when they halted me in front of a Russian truck, which was used to transport me to Hanoi. During the ride they kept me face down, which allowed me to staunch the flow of blood from my face and arm. The ride itself seemed to last less than an hour. They stopped in front of an old French building of large size and allowed me to sit up in the early morning twilight. I was then unceremoniously pushed off the truck flatbed, falling about six feet to the pavement, where I suffered a shoulder separation. I was unable to move from where I had landed, and was then dragged by two soldiers into the prison yard of what I was to discover was the Hanoi Hilton.

December 22, day five of the operation, called for a change of tactics. As SAC had seen in the carnage of day three, the North Vietnamese had read a pattern in the earlier Linebacker attacks. The time had come to use the lesson of SAC's earlier mistakes against the enemy. Thirty B–52Ds from the 307th BW took off from U Tapao and approached Hanoi from the south over the Gulf of Tonkin. About fifty miles from Hanoi, the lead cells made a sudden right turn toward Hai-

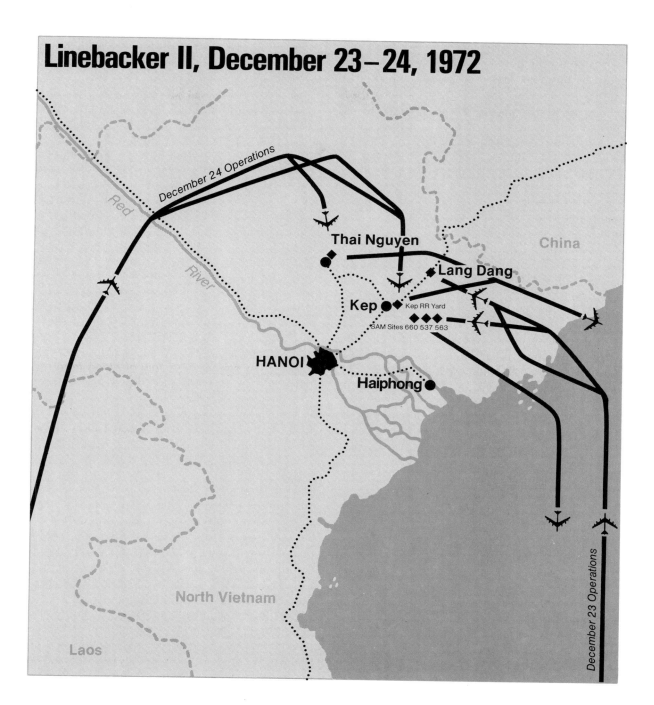

Linebacker II, December 23–24, 1972

December 24 Operations

Red

River

China

Thai Nguyen

Lang Dang

Kep — Kep RR Yard

SAM Sites 660 537 563

HANOI

Haiphong

North Vietnam

Laos

December 23 Operations

phong. Less than ten minutes later petroleum tank farms and rail facilities across Haiphong were exploding in balls of fire and black smoke. The surprised defenders managed to fire forty-three SAMs, but the entire bomber force emerged unscathed.

The following night, December 23, was a replay of both the mission and the success of the twenty-second. Again, thirty bombers, eighteen from U Tapao and a dozen from Andersen, went in, feinted toward Hanoi, and hit another target; again, thirty bombers emerged sans battle damage. The principal target this night was the Lang Dang rail yards forty-five miles northwest of Hanoi on one of the main lines out of China. Also on the list, however, were three SAM batteries near Kep, about thirty miles due west of Hanoi's northern suburbs. The reason for knocking out the SAM batteries, which weren't even in position to harass bombers en route to Lang Dang, would not be clear until three nights later. The mission of December 24, Christmas Eve, repeated the scenario of the previous two. Once again, thirty bombers, this time all from U Tapao, went out, struck rail yards away from Hanoi, and returned unharmed. The latter is remarkable, considering that the bombers flew across the northernmost and widest part of North Vietnam. Two of the cells were attacked unsuccessfully by MiGs, with one of them, a more advanced MiG-21, being shot down by tail gunner A1c. Albert Moore in Ruby 3. (Moore was one of two B-52 tail gunners to get a confirmed MiG kill during the war, the other being Sgt. Samuel Turner on December 18, the first night of Linebacker II.)

With the missions of December 22–24, SAC was allowing the enemy to observe a new pattern emerging in the attack scenario. They had been given the new pattern, but because the attacks were against unpredictable targets, they had lost the ability to lie in wait with their most potent defenses. The new scenario, which confused and infuriated the North Vietnamese, also successfully avoided aircraft losses during the three days leading up to Christmas.

On Christmas Day, the entire B-52 force paused for a twenty-four-hour halt in what the world press was now calling "the Christmas bombings." While the big bombers were idle, the crews, both air and ground, were anything but. Plans were proceeding apace for what would be the biggest B-52 attack of the war. On the night of December 26, flying from both U Tapao and Andersen, 120 B-52s in ten waves would attack Thai Nguyen, Haiphong, and seven separate target complexes in Hanoi. Unlike the earlier hundred plane raids, which were spread out over several hours, the entire December 26 force would hit their targets between half past eight and quarter to nine. The enemy defenses would be taxed to the limit; downtown Hanoi, for example, would be attacked simultaneously by four separate waves coming from four separate directions. For SAC and Eighth Air Force planners, it was an incredible chore to coordinate such a complex operation. Split-second timing would have to be accurately calculated, then accurately flown.

It was a scene tailor-made for Hollywood: The largest B-52 operation in history. A Russian trawler (read spy ship) sitting offshore watching the bombers take off from Guam. A transport plane making an emergency landing in the middle of the launch of tankers at Kadena, costing the refueling planes a quarter of an hour. Lt. Col. George Allison, in the third wave out of Andersen, recalled that the planes from Guam had to have the gas.

Now the situation was a mess. A smooth-flowing stream of bombers, coming in from the east, was scheduled to meet a like stream of tankers moving in from the north [Kadena], in predetermined groupings at predetermined times over a

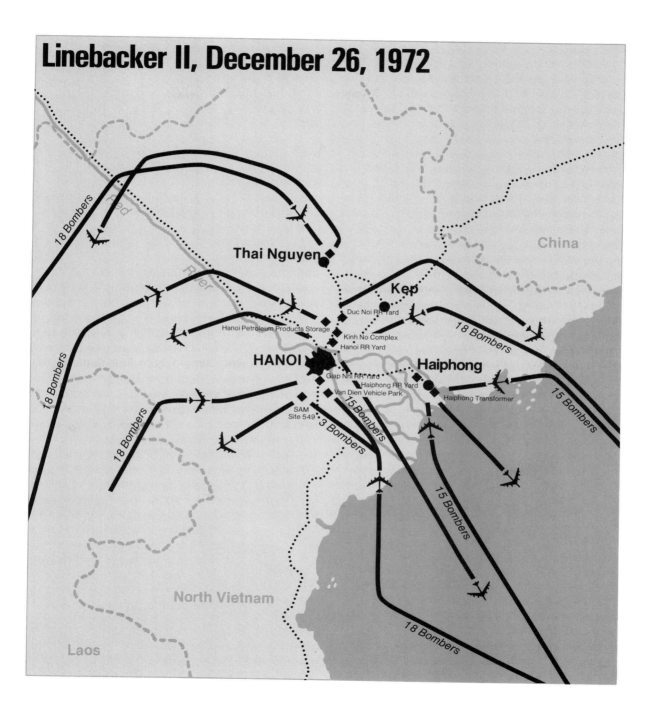

Linebacker II, December 26, 1972

Thai Nguyen

Kep

Duc Noi RR Yard

Kinh No Complex

Hanoi Petroleum Products Storage

Hanoi RR Yard

HANOI

Giap Nhi RR Yard

Haiphong

Haiphong RR Yard

Van Dien Vehicle Park

Haiphong Transformer

SAM Site 549

China

North Vietnam

Laos

Red River

18 Bombers

18 Bombers

18 Bombers

18 Bombers

18 Bombers

15 Bombers

15 Bombers

15 Bombers

3 Bombers

15 Bombers

18 Bombers

specific point in the ocean. Only now there was a fifteen-minute discrepancy in arrival times.

In a well-coordinated move, each cell within the wave began a series of airspeed and course adjustments to compensate for the problem, systematically relaying this action backwards and forwards in the stream, and passing it to the tanker force. The aircraft would now theoretically meet at the adjusted points and times, but the problem did not end there.

For one thing, the principle of effecting an in-flight rendezvous contains elements of geometry and algebra, wherein the physical act is an artful blending of mathematical inputs. Except that, now, many of the entering arguments had changed. Speeds and angular relationships were no longer according to plan. They varied substantially from the norm in most cases. This meant for many crews that it all boiled down to each individual cell of aircraft, be it bomber or tanker, having to improvise their navigation to be where they said they would be, when they said they'd be there.

At first consideration, it would appear that the electronic capabilities of both types of aircraft to monitor one another's position would obviate such a problem. That, unfortunately, was not the case. For, in the confusion of the timing conflict, the natural drive for each cell to join up with its counterpart, and the close spacing of all cells, the resulting electronic rendezvous signals being emitted from the many aircraft literally saturated the scene. The rendezvous beacon signal was transmitted at a common frequency, and the result was that a radar scope might easily record twelve or more individual signals at one time. To put it in the jargon of the trade, it looked as though someone had dumped a bag of popcorn all over the scope.

However, in spite of the pressure and consternation which the timing disparity had created, all rendezvous were consistently effected and the needed fuel transferred.

With the total B–52 force scheduled over all targets inside of a fifteen-minute time span, timing was critical, and the operation was running fifteen minutes behind schedule. Fortunately, the mission planners had designed a "time control box," an accordian-like flight path off the coast of South Vietnam that allowed the bombers to catch up to one another by condensing the flight path of the first cells. Once re-formed, the bombers headed north in close formation, in radio silence, with the only thing visible in the dark being the red lights on the tops of the fuselages. One pilot likened it to a highway at night.

. . . nothing but a stream of upper rotating beacons as far as I could see. It was sort of eerie, too, once we went into radio silence procedures. Nothing was said, but each aircraft was flashing an "I'm here" to his buddies. Then it occurred to me that we would be meeting a whole bunch more of the force, which was coming up using a route over the land mass. As many of us as there were, the U Tapao troops were also going to be there in strength. At that moment, it dawned on me just how special this night was.

Colonel McCarthy, leading the first wave, recalled:

As they headed north over the Gulf of Tonkin, I heard Tom Lebar call in that his wave was at the join-up point on time and that the wave was compressed. They had done one hell of a fine job.

When we crossed the 17th parallel, we were committed. That was the last point at which I or higher headquarters could recall the forces. From here until the target area we would be using radio silence procedures. The only radio call allowed would be if you got jumped by a MiG and you needed MiG CAP support.

As Haiphong passed off our left wing, we could see that the Navy support forces were really working over the SAM and AAA sites. The whole area was lit up like a Christmas tree. We could hear Red Crown issuing SAM and MiG warnings to the friendly aircraft over Haiphong. We hoped that this activity would divert their attention from our G-model bombers, who would soon be arriving. Even though they weren't going to downtown Hanoi anymore, they were headed for the port city. As we all knew, that was plenty tough duty.

We coasted in northeast of Haiphong and headed for our IP, where we would turn southwest toward Hanoi. The IP turned out to be in the same area that Marty Fulcher had led the BUFFs on the twenty-third against the SAM sites that had the reputation of being such lousy shots.

The flak started coming up when we made our first landfall. Once again, we were most vividly aware of the heavy, black, ugly explosions which characterized the 100mm. Even at night, the black smoke from these explosions is visible. Since we were at a lower altitude than we had flown before, our wave would be more vulnerable to this AAA than on most previous missions. Close to the IP the flak became more intense and the explosions were closer to the aircraft. . . .

Then the SAMs really started coming. It was apparent this was no F Troop doing the aiming. The missiles lifted off and headed for the aircraft. As we had long ago learned to do, we fixed our attention on those which maintained their same relative position even as we maneuvered. All of the first six missiles fired appeared to maintain their same relative position in the windshield. Then A1c. Ken Schell reported from the tail that he had three more SAMs at six o'clock heading for us. The next few minutes were going to be interesting.

Now that the whole force was committed and we were on the bomb run, I had nothing to do until after bombs away, so I decided to count the SAMs launched against us. Out the copilot's window, Lt. Ron Thomas reported four more coming up on the right side and two at his one o'clock position. Bill reported three more on the left side as the first six started exploding. Some were close—too close for comfort.

Listening to the navigation team on interphone downstairs, you would have thought they were making a practice bomb run back in the States. The checklist was unhurried. Capt. Joe Gangwish, the radar navigator, calmly discussed the identification of the aiming point that they were using for this bomb run with his teammate, Major Francis.

About 100 seconds prior to bombs away, the cockpit lit up like it was daylight. The light came from the rocket exhaust of a SAM that had come up right under the nose. The EW had reported an extremely strong signal, and he was right. It's hard to judge miss distance at night, but that one looked like it missed us by less than fifty feet. The proximity fuse should have detonated the warhead, but it didn't. Somebody upstairs was looking after us that night.

After twenty-six SAMs I quit counting. They were coming up too fast to count. It appeared in the cockpit as if they were now barraging SAMs in order to make the lead element of the wave turn from its intended course.

Just . . . prior to bombs away, the formation stopped maneuvering to provide the required gyro stabilization to the bombing computers. Regardless of how close the SAMs appeared, the bomber had to remain straight and level.

One crew during the raids actually saw a SAM that was going to hit them when they were only seconds away from bomb release. The copilot calmly announced the impending impact to the crew over interphone. The aircraft dropped its bombs on target and was hit moments later. That's what I call "guts football."

At bombs away, it looked like we were right in the middle of a fireworks factory that was in the process of blowing up. The radio was completely saturated with SAM calls and MiG warnings. As the bomb doors closed, several SAMs exploded nearby. Others could be seen arcing over and starting a descent, then detonating. If the proximity fuse didn't find a target, SA–2s were set to self-destruct at the end of a predetermined time interval.

Our computer's "bombs away" signal went to the bomb bay right on the time track. Despite the SAMs and the 100-knot headwinds, the nav team had dropped their bombs on target at the exact second called for in the frag order.

Some minutes afterwards, as we were departing the immediate Hanoi area, there was a brilliant explosion off to our left rear that lit up the whole sky for miles around. A B–52D (Ebony 2) had been hit and had exploded in midair. Momentarily, the radios went silent. Everyone was listening for the emergency beepers that are automatically activated when a parachute opens. We could make out two, or possibly three, different beepers going off. Miraculously, four of the Kincheloe Air Force Base, Michigan, crew escaped the aircraft, becoming POWs. Then there was a call from another aircraft, Ash 1, stating that he had been hit and was heading for the water. The pilot reported that he was losing altitude and he was having difficulty controlling the aircraft. Red Crown started vectoring F–4s to escort the crippled bomber to safety. . . .

Now came an equally hard part—sweating out the time until the entire bomber stream had dropped their bombs and the cell leaders reported their losses. From the congestion on the radios, it was apparent that the North Vietnamese had loaded up plenty of missiles and were using them.

Suddenly, one of the cells in our wave reported MiGs closing in and requested fighter support. Red Crown, who had been working with Ash 1, started vectoring other F–4s to the BUFF under possible attack. I gave the command for all upper rotating beacons and all taillights to be turned off. As the F–4s approached, the MiG apparently broke off his attack, because the fighters couldn't locate him and the target disappeared from the gunners' radars. This appeared to be another one of those cases where the MiGs were pacing the B–52s for the SAM gunners. . . .

Finally, the last cell had exited the threat zones and reported in. The customary expression of this was, "So and so cell, out with three." A more picturesque expression, which sort of captured what was happening, was when a formation reported themselves "over the fence with three." Except for the violent loss of Ebony 2 and the problems Ash 1 was still having, the rest of the force was intact. Considering what had just happened, their successive reports of "out with three" were heartlifting.

Of 113 bombers who arrived over the target, only 2 had been lost to SAMs. The SAM batteries that had been bombed by B–52s on the twenty-third may have not been on the route to the primary target then, but their absence may well have saved some lives on the twenty-sixth. Electronic countermeasures had also been refined by teams working around the clock since the first missions. Indeed, no aircraft had been lost from a three-plane cell. The two that were lost had been from cells whose third member had been forced to turn back prior to arriving over the target.

The North Vietnamese were worried. They realized that the turning point had arrived. The Eighth Air Force, which had destroyed the war-making power of the mighty German Reich twenty-seven years earlier, was now flying into the most heavily defended corridor ever encountered by a strategic air offensive and emerging with less than two percent losses. Reconnaissance photos showed that the targets marked for the twenty-sixth had been virtually obliterated.

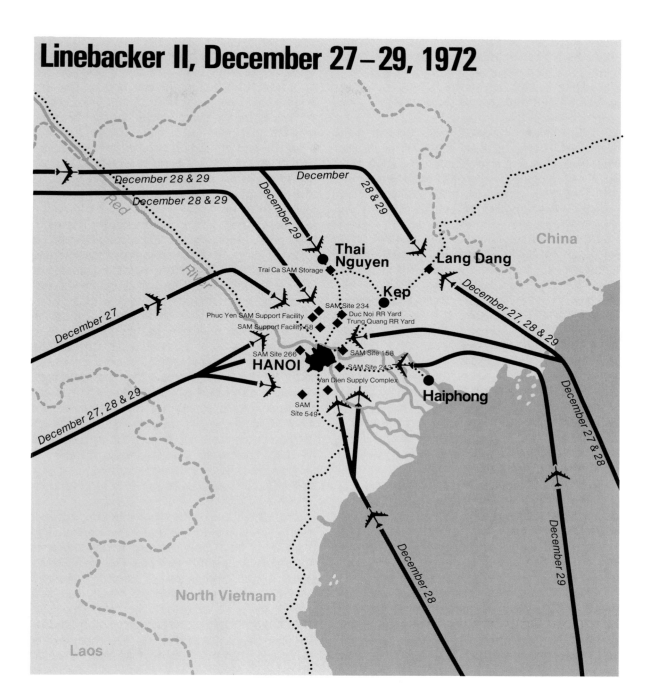

Linebacker II, December 27–29, 1972

December 28 & 29

December 28 & 29

December 29

December 28 & 29

Thai Nguyen

Lang Dang

Trai Ca SAM Storage

Kep

December 27

SAM Site 234

Phuc Yen SAM Support Facility

Duc Noi RR Yard

Trung Quang RR Yard

SAM Support Facility 58

December 27, 28 & 29

SAM Site 266

SAM Site 158

HANOI

SAM Site 243

Van Dien Supply Complex

December 27, 28 & 29

Haiphong

SAM Site 549

China

December 27 & 28

Red River

December 28

December 29

North Vietnam

Laos

117

The attack on the night of the twenty-seventh was similar, though with half the number of bombers divided three ways between Lang Dang and supply dumps, rail yards, and SAM batteries on the north and south sides of Hanoi. The targets between the latter two had been pretty well eliminated the night before. Mission planners called for all sixty of the bombers to release their bombs in a ten-minute time span. That night, if any plane had to drop out of the three-plane cell, the two remaining B–52s would form up with another cell to create a five-plane cell for ECM protection.

It was a night marked by the most erratic SAM launches yet encountered, and by two launches that were anything but erratic. Most of the SAMs went wide by as much as half a mile, but the number 2 in Ash Cell out of U Tapao, late of Ellsworth AFB, South Dakota, took a near-direct hit moments after it had destroyed another SAM battery just as its missiles left the ground. Capt. John Mize managed to hold the crippled wreck together long enough to ditch over Laos, where the entire crew were rescued.

The crew of the lead BUFF in Cobalt Cell wasn't so lucky. Just a hair short of Trung Quang rail yard, the plane flew into a wall of SAMs. The bomber reeled out of control, bay doors jammed. Most of the crew was able to get out alive, with all but two checking into the Hanoi Hilton for the duration. The North Vietnamese had taken two of the sixty December 27 bombers, but it was clear by the erratic launches that the defense net had broken down. Cobalt 1 would be the last B–52 lost in combat in Southeast Asia.

The attack plan for the twenty-eighth kept up the pressure. Again, sixty sorties were flown, with a third hitting Lang Dang again and the rest going downtown. Lang Dang was the principal choke point on the main rail line leading in from China, which made it a key strategic objective. The missions were successful and flown without a loss. The SAM count was down, and none of the bombers encountered any MiGs. It began to seem that the only problem left facing the Eighth Air Force mission planners was finding strategic targets that had not already been pulverized.

The raid on the twenty-eighth was followed by another sixty-plane raid the next day. By now everyone from the ground crews to the planners had fallen into the routine required to launch missions day in and day out indefinitely. Even as the bombers of the twenty-eighth were returning and those of the twenty-ninth being readied for their visits to the Phuc Yen, Thai Nguyen, and Lang Dang, the planners were putting together the mission for the night of the thirtieth.

That raid was destined never to be flown. Colonel McCarthy recalled that as the crews filed into the briefing room on the twenty-ninth for what would be the final Linebacker II briefing, he could sense their rising level of confidence.

We were closing in for the finale, and they knew it. The rumor had started floating around that this might be the last day of the big raids, and they wanted to be a part of it. I had crews who had just landed hours earlier from the previous night's mission ask to be put in the lineup. Crews who had been designated as spares argued emphatically as to why they should be designated as primary crews, rather than spare.

The launch went flawlessly. By now the launch of a thirty-plane mission had become a rather routine affair, but there was something about them that always drew a crowd. For this launch, there must have been at least eight thousand spectators along the flight line and gathered at vantage points on buildings. Sensing the end, offices all over the base closed down to let their people see it.

The last bomb of Linebacker II fell at seventeen minutes before midnight on December 29, 1972, bringing to a close the most intensive strategic air offensive since World War II. It was the last B–52 mission north of the 20th parallel. One and a half million pounds of bombs had been dropped in 729 missions, with devastating effect. The enemy had fired somewhere between 884 and 1,242 SAMs, with only 15 B–52s shot down. In their wake, the bombers left nearly all of North Vietnam's electricity generating capacity in shambles, and a quarter of its petroleum reserves destroyed. Rail lines had been cut in five hundred places with several hundred engines and railcars put out of business. Though Hanoi and Haiphong felt the brunt of Linebacker II, perhaps the most telling effect was felt half a world away at the Paris peace talks, where on January 24, 1973, the U.S. negotiator Dr. Henry Kissinger remarked that "there was a deadlock in the middle of December, and there was a rapid movement when negotiations resumed on January 8. These facts have to be analyzed by each person for himself."

Three days later the North Vietnamese signed the long-elusive peace treaty.

Although in the shadow of an operation like Linebacker II almost any operation is anticlimactic, the Arc Light missions did continue. The last B–52 missions against both South Vietnam and North Vietnam (south of the 20th parallel) were flown on January 27, 1973, the same day that the Paris peace accords were signed. The last B–52 missions over Laos were flown in mid-April. The BUFFs continued to fly missions over Cambodia against the rebel forces advancing on Phnom Penh until they were halted by the congressional ban on bombing; the last B–52 sortie in Southeast Asia was flown there on August 15.

SAC KC–135s also flew their last combat support missions during August, marking an end to nine years and two months of SAC operations in the war in Southeast Asia. During that time, the tankers transferred nearly a billion and a half gallons of fuel in 194,687 sorties and 813,878

Linebacker II

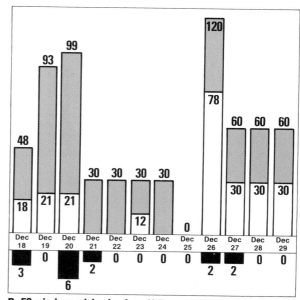

B–52 missions originating from U Tapao RTNAB, Thailand ▨
B–52 missions originating from Andersen AFB, Guam ☐
Total B–52s lost on each date ■

aerial refuelings. On December 21, 1975, eleven and a half years after the first Yankee Team tanker operations and eight months after they provided support for the final withdrawal from Saigon, the last seventeen KC–135s left U Tapao and Southeast Asia for the last time.

Linebacker II did not end the war. What it did do was twofold: first, the operation proved once again that strategic airpower had the potential to be the decisive factor in the defeat of an enemy; secondly, it drove the North Vietnamese to seek a ceasefire and sufficiently throttled their war-making capabilities so that they were unable to launch a decisive offensive for more than two years. Linebacker II proved that the United States could have won the war in Southeast Asia had they chosen to fight it as a war and not as a bloody experiment in protracted, sub-limited war.

Part V
SAC in an Uncertain World

19 The Other Strategic Air Commands

SAC is not an isolated entity. It exists today in a world inhabited by other nations with strategic ambitions, strategic nuclear weapons, and strategic air commands.

During World War II, the only nations capable of carrying out a sustained, integrated strategic air offensive were Britain, the United States, and to a certain extent, Germany, although they lacked a strategic bomber. Both the Japanese and the Russians concentrated almost entirely on tactical aircraft for tactical air warfare, although the Japanese did develop some long-range seaplanes. After the war the Americans promptly set about developing a new generation of strategic bombers—the jet-assisted Consolidated B–36 and Boeing's B–47 and B–52. The British turned to the same plane makers that had provided their wartime heavy bombers and took delivery of the V bombers, the Vickers Valiant, the Handley Page Victor, and the Avro Vulcan.

The Russians became converts to the idea of strategic airpower when they occupied Germany after the war and witnessed firsthand the effectiveness of the Anglo-American stra-

tegic air offensive. Their first venture into the realm of strategic aircraft took place by way of several American B–29 Superfortress strategic bombers that had made forced landings at Vladivostok after raids on Japan toward the end of the war. The Soviet Union was an American ally against Germany but was neutral in the war against Japan (having been twice beaten by the Japanese in the preceding half-century). Thus, recognizing the importance of the B–29s, the Russians interned the big bombers rather than turning them back to the Americans. The confiscated Superforts were turned over to the Tupolev design bureau, who disassembled them and duplicated their every detail, producing several hundred Russian "B–29s" under the Tupolev designation Tu–4. Over the years since, Tupolev has been responsible for nearly all the Soviet strategic bombers.

Turning the clock ahead forty years, we find over 140 nations with air forces but still only a handful with true strategic airpower capabilities. Of the nations possessing nuclear weapons, both India and Israel would depend on tactical aircraft of relatively short range to deliver them, although it is certain that if either nation resorted to nuclear warfare, the targets would be strategic. It is ironic that one of the only true strategic bombing missions (with conventional weapons) flown by the Israeli Air Force in its many wars was in 1981 against the Osirik nuclear reactor site in Iraq, which was allegedly building nuclear weapons, not only for Israel's

Left: A TAC Phantom intercepts a Soviet Tu-95 Bear bomber. Bombers of the Dal'naya Aviatsiya (the Russian SAC) continuously probe American air space.

traditional enemies in the Arab world, but for India's traditional enemy, Pakistan, as well.

The People's Republic of China, the first non-Western nation to carry out nuclear weapons testing (1964) has several hundred such weapons stockpiled and the makings of a triad of delivery systems. The Chinese strategic triad is divided among their army, navy, and air force with their missile force, called Second Artillery, being assigned to army control. The Second Artillery has fewer than a half dozen ICBMs but over a hundred IRBMs and MRBMs with sufficient range to hit targets either in the Soviet Union or elsewhere in Asia. Chinese strategic airpower rests in three regiments totaling ninety Hong-6 medium bombers (Chinese versions of the Tupolev Tu–16), although many tactical aircraft are probably nuclear capable. For the Chinese, submarine-launched ballistic missiles are a recent innovation, and only a couple of experimental missile subs have been launched.

Britain, America's partner in the big strategic air offensive of the forties and possessor of a

Above: The British Vulcan bomber was in the RAF for thirty years but didn't fly a combat mission until the year before it was retired, when it went to war in the Falklands.

nuclear arsenal since 1952, no longer has, as of 1983, long-range strategic capability remaining within its Royal Air Force. The last of the RAF's V series of strategic bombers, the Avro Vulcans, were retired in 1983 after three decades and after having flown their only strategic bombing missions just the year before. In 1982 the Vulcans had been on the verge of retirement (the Victors had earlier been converted to air-refueling tankers) when Argentina invaded the Falkland Islands. In order to launch an invasion to recapture the Falklands, the British needed to gain air superiority, which would require knocking out the airfield at Stanley. The Vulcans were selected for this mission, which would be flown from the British advanced base on Ascension Island, 3,400 miles from the Falklands. The Vulcans flew a series of single-plane raids that were the first strategic bomber missions since SAC's participation in Linebacker II ten years earlier, the longest actual combat missions ever flown by strategic bombers and the last ever in the long history of Britain's Royal Air Force. With the swan song of the Vulcan, Britain's strategic nuclear strike force consists only of four *Resolution*-class nuclear submarines, each armed with sixteen Polaris three-MIRV missiles.

France was the fourth nation to acquire nuclear weapons (1960) and is the only nation other than the two superpowers, and maybe China, to have developed a triad. France withdrew from the military command of NATO in 1966 and has since been determined to develop its own independent strategic forces. France has six nuclear submarines, each equipped with sixteen M–20 missiles and an experimental diesel with four missile tubes. The land-based leg of the French triad consists of eighteen silo-based S–3 intermediate-range missiles and six strategic bomber squadrons equipped with thirty-four Dassault-Breguet Mirage IV bombers. The latter are delta-winged supersonic aircraft (Mach 2.2) slightly larger than SAC's FB–111, with nearly identical speed and range. The Mirage IV is aerial refuelable giving the French Armée de l'air Commandement des Forces Aériennes Stratégique (Strategic Air Command) more than sufficient range to reach targets in the Soviet Union.

The Soviet Union's triad is under the operational control of the Soviet navy and, not one, but two, strategic air commands. The naval leg of their triad includes eighty-three subs armed with 989 missiles. The Russian air force, unlike its American counterpart, is actually three services rather than one. There are the Strategic Rocket Forces, the Troops of Air Defense (Protivo-Vozdoshnaya Oborona Strany, or PVO-Strany), and the Soviet Air Force (Voenno-Vozdushnye Sily, or VVS). In turn, the latter contains within it the Air Transport Command (Voenno-Transportnaya), a tactical air command

called Frontal Aviation (Frontovaya Aviatsiya), and Long-Range Aviation (Dal'naya Aviatsiya, or DA).

Within this command structure, it is the Strategic Rocket Forces and Long-Range Aviation that parallel the mission performed by SAC. The Strategic Rocket Forces maintain an inventory of 1,398 ICBMs, including 308 of the huge SS–18s (Soviet designation RS–20), which at 104 feet are the largest Soviet ICBMs and one foot longer than SAC's Titans. The arsenal also includes 310 of the 75-foot SS–19 (Soviet designation RS–18), the most modern of the Russian ICBMs, most of them in a six-warhead configuration. In addition to the ICBMs, the Strategic Rocket Forces have operational control of an estimated 606 IRBMs and MRBMs, five hundred of them deployed in the western USSR within striking range of Western Europe and the rest deployed within range of China. More than half of these are the new mobile SS–20 with its reloadable launchers.

Long-Range Aviation (DA) operates about 640 strategic bombers organized into three bomber corps or air armies, two opposite NATO and one in the far east opposite China. The most well known of DA's heavy bombers is the Tupolev Tu–95 (NATO code name Bear). In service since 1955, the Bear has proven to be one of the most successful warplanes designed in the Soviet Union. The huge bomber uniquely combines a swept-wing configuration with turboprop power plants to achieve a speed and performance level comparable to many jets (transports included) of its size and weight class, even jets of much more modern design. Because of its maximum range of over 10,000 miles, the Bear has been adapted for a maritime reconnaissance role and is frequently encountered off the coast of the southeastern United States on its regular recon runs between the Soviet Union and Cuba. In May 1980, the Soviet Union signed a treaty with the Marxist government of the Caribbean island na-

tion of Grenada permitting Bears to operate out of the airport being built by Cuba at Point Salines on Grenada. The completed airport was an object of the American invasion three years later.

The other long-range heavy bomber in DA service is the Myasishchev M–4 (NATO code name Bison). The only bomber in DA service that was not a product of the Tupolev design bureau, the Bison is a four-turbojet bomber in the same size and weight class as the Bear and SAC's B–52. Making its debut in the early fifties at the same time as the Bear and the B–52, the Bison has not been nearly as successful as either. The range of the Bison is about half that of the other two; its speed is greater than that of the Bear and about the same as the B–52. The bomb capacity of the Bison is about fifteen tons compared with about twelve tons for the Bear, both much less than the B–52. Among the reasons for the lack of the Bison's success is certainly its limited range, but also its landing gear design, which causes the aircraft to sit low to the ground, preventing the mounting of air-to-ground missiles and other ordnance under the fuselage or wings. Many Bisons have been converted to air-refueling tankers and reconnaissance air-

craft, and it is reasonable to assume that the DA no longer uses them as bombers.

The long-range heavy bombers of DA, like the B–52 of SAC, served from the mid-fifties to the mid-eighties without a successor, but DA's medium bombers have continued to proliferate. Currently there are about 150 heavy bombers in DA, 105 of them Bears. Meanwhile, there are over 535 medium bombers, including 310 of the old twin-jet Tupolev Tu–16s (NATO code name Badger), which are in the same size and weight class as SAC's long-retired B–47. The Tu–16 made its appearance in 1952 shortly after the B–47.

The DA mediums also include 125 twin-jet Tupolev Tu–22s (NATO code name Blinder). The Blinder was designed in the late fifties at the same time and for the same reason that SAC was developing its supersonic B–58. Both the Badger and the B–47 were, because of modest speed and range, becoming obsolete in their role as strategic bombers able to penetrate to heavily defended strategic targets. Rated at about Mach 1.5, the Blinder is slower, although larger, than

the B–58 was. It has a slightly shorter range than the B–58 and a bit less bomb capacity. Unlike the B–58, though, the Blinder is still in service with DA as well as having been exported to Iraq and Libya, where it may be operated by Russian crews.

The most recent of DA medium bombers, and one that the American negotiators at the SALT II arms talks wanted to see classed as a long-range heavy bomber, is Tupolev's Tu–22M (NATO designation TU–26, code name Backfire). The Backfire is a Mach 2 variable-geometry strategic bomber in roughly the same size and weight class as SAC's B–1. Both had their origins in the middle to late sixties, but unlike the B–1, the Backfire was considered a high-priority project and it was in DA service by the mid-seventies. The International Institute for

Above: Soviet maintenance men at work on a Tu-22 "Blinder-A" supersonic jet bomber.

Strategic Studies in London lists the number of Backfires at 100 in 1982, but other reports indicate that between 150 and 200 were in service with DA by that time, with annual production rated at between 35 and 42 airplanes.

The Backfire is easily the most formidable bomber presently in DA inventory. Its speed is twice that of the B–1B and comparable to that of many contemporary Western interceptors. Its internal bomb capacity is estimated at around thirteen tons, but it has been observed with external weapons pylons under its fuselage and it has been designed to carry one or perhaps two AS–4 (NATO code name Kitchen) Mach 2 air-to-surface missiles similar to SAC's SRAM or

125

Comparative Strategic Bomber Strengths

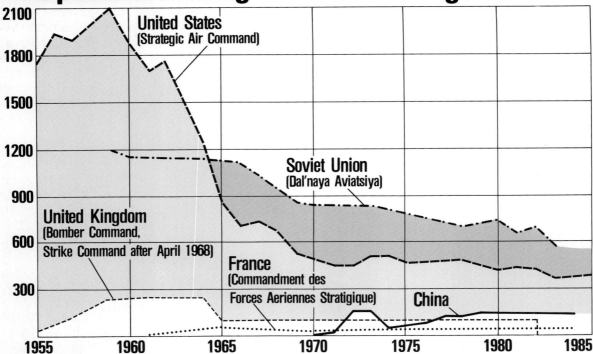

ALCM. The Kitchen, which can also be carried by both the Bear and the Blinder has been in use by DA since the sixties and is nearly twice as long as the ALCM, with a much shorter range of under two hundred miles.

The range of the Backfire is in the medium bomber category, but it is aerial-refuelable, giving it an intercontinental capability. It was for this reason that the American negotiators tried to get it included in SALT II, unsuccessfully. The Backfire was such a point of controversy that Soviet President Brezhnev handed the following written note to American President Carter on June 16, 1979, when they met face to face two days prior to the signing of the SALT II treaty in Vienna:

The Soviet side informs the U.S. side that the Soviet "Tu–22M" airplane, called "Backfire" in the U.S.A., is a medium-range bomber, and that it does not intend to give this airplane the capability of operating at intercontinental distances. In this connection, the Soviet side states that it will not increase the radius of action of this airplane in such a way as to enable it to strike targets on the territory of the U.S.A. Nor does it intend to give it such a capability in any other manner, including by in-flight refueling. At the same time, the Soviet side states that it will not increase the production rate of this airplane as compared to the present rate.

When the note was made public, American Secretary of State Cyrus Vance added,
President Brezhnev confirmed that the Soviet

Backfire production rate would not exceed thirty per year. President Carter stated that the United States enters into the SALT II Agreement on the basis of the commitments contained in the Soviet statement and that it considers the carrying out of these commitments to be essential to the obligations assumed under the Treaty.

Two years later John W. R. Taylor, editor of *Jane's All the World's Aircraft* reported in the *Soviet Aerospace Almanac* that

there is no longer any need to leave the in-flight refueling noseprobe at home when flying Backfire over international waters; this was done to stress the peripheral/theater range capability which excluded the aircraft from SALT II restrictions. Nobody doubts any longer that Backfire does have an intercontinental capability which will be enhanced as its engines are developed. Production was to be limited to a rate of 30 per year by SALT II and is said to have been stepped up to 42 per year following non-ratification of the Treaty.

While the international controversy over the Backfire and the domestic controversy over the future of the B–1 were raging, the Tupolev designers were hard at work on still another strategic bomber, this one even more sophisticated than the Backfire. The new plane was first photographed at the Soviet flight test center at Ramenskoye in November of 1981 and was given the NATO code name Blackjack in 1983. What is known about this new Tupolev long-range bomber is cause for alarm. What immediately astounded analysts about the Blackjack was its size. It is not only 40 percent larger than the Backfire and 20 percent larger than the B–1, it is longer (though with shorter wingspan) by up to 20 feet than either the B–36 or B–52, which were the largest combat aircraft ever in service. With its enormous size comes a correspondingly large weapons capacity, which will probably include the new SS–NX–21 cruise missile that is

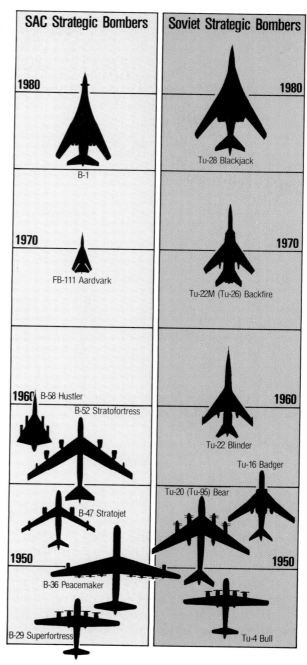

SAC Strategic Bombers

1980 — B-1

1970 — FB-111 Aardvark

1960 — B-58 Hustler / B-52 Stratofortress / B-47 Stratojet

1950 — B-36 Peacemaker / B-29 Superfortress

Soviet Strategic Bombers

1980 — Tu-28 Blackjack

1970 — Tu-22M (Tu-26) Backfire

1960 — Tu-22 Blinder / Tu-16 Badger / Tu-20 (Tu-95) Bear

1950 — Tu-4 Bull

also being developed for DA. The Blackjack is, like the Backfire and B–1, a variable-geometry aircraft, giving it the enhanced flexibility and performance required by a modern strategic bomber. The performance will also be enhanced by four Koliesov turbojet engines that were designed for the Tu–144 supersonic airliner. These engines would allow the Blackjack to cruise for long distances at Mach 2, whereas most combat aircraft cruise below the speed of sound to save fuel and extend their range. Thus the new bomber would probably have an "over-the-target dash" capability at speeds well above Mach 2 and range approaching that of the Bear and B–52 even if it *did* conserve its fuel.

The Blackjack is expected to enter operational service around the same time as the B–1B, in 1986 or thereabouts. Its deployment, complementing the Backfires then in service, will give DA a decided qualitative *and* quantitative advantage over SAC's bomber forces. If its deployment is delayed, the B–1B will be the world's superior strategic bomber, though the B–1B will be well outnumbered by DA's Backfires.

20 Strategic Arms Control

Nuclear weaponry emerged as an American monopoly after World War II, but that condition changed with the first detonation of a nuclear device by Russia. Since then, these two superpowers have been joined by Great Britain in 1952, France in 1960, the People's Republic of China in 1964, and India a decade later, with Israel (and possibly South Africa) probably nuclear capable since the early seventies, although they have conducted no detectable tests.

Even after the United States lost its monopoly of nuclear weapons to the Russians in 1949, it continued to be superior to the Soviet Union in terms of the number of bombs in its arsenal. SAC aircraft were, throughout the late forties and most of the fifties, both quantitatively and qualitatively superior to what was available to the Soviets. Furthermore, the United States had bases from which SAC bombers could strike deep into the Soviet Union, and the Russians lacked a corresponding capability. What the Russians *did* have was an enormous conventional army that outnumbered Western forces in Europe. The United States lacked the conventional power to match the Soviets and maintained its nuclear capability to counterbalance the Soviet threat to Europe. At the same time, however, the Russians were rapidly building up their nuclear capability. They were four years behind the Americans in detonating an atomic bomb, but only a year behind the Americans when they exploded their first hydrogen bomb in 1953. By the late fifties they had launched the first intercontinental ballistic missile and had beaten the Americans into outer space with their *Sputnik* satellite.

By the mid-sixties the Soviet nuclear arsenal had been expanded to the point where it eclipsed American nuclear superiority. But as late as 1965, the U.S. secretary of defense still felt that "the Soviets have decided they have lost the quantitative [nuclear arms] race, and they are not seeking to engage us in that contest. There is no indication that the Soviets are seeking to develop a strategic nuclear force as large as ours." McNamara called for a self-imposed ceiling on the American strategic arsenal at a level where it could achieve "Assured Destruction" of a third of the population of the USSR and two thirds of its industry. McNamara's assessment of Russian intentions and capabilities was recognized as incorrect, however, when the Russians achieved parity with and then surpassed the

Americans in the arms race, bringing about a condition of "*Mutual* Assured Destruction," with its appropriate acronym, MAD.

In 1962, the most climactic moment in the nuclear arms race came with the Soviet introduction of ballistic missiles into Cuba. President John Kennedy found himself staring into the abyss of nuclear war. He considered the options that could be taken, such as launching a first strike against the Soviet Union, invading Cuba, or nothing. When he spoke to the nation on the night of October 22, he had decided to blockade Cuba and give the Russians a chance, short of war, to reverse their actions.

"My fellow citizens," Kennedy began, "let no one doubt that this is a difficult and dangerous effort on which we have set out. No one can foresee precisely what course it will take, but the greatest danger of all would be to do nothing. The nineteen-thirties taught us a clear lesson: aggressive conduct, if allowed to go unchecked and unchallenged, ultimately leads to war." In his speech, Kennedy was paraphrasing Thomas Jefferson, who nearly two centuries before had said, "Weakness provokes insult and injury while a condition to punish often prevents it."

The Russians withdrew their missiles, and the world backed away from the brink of nuclear holocaust. The deterrent effect of the SAC arsenal had worked, and the nation breathed easier, praying the world would never come that close again.

The Cuban missile crisis clearly illustrated the dangers of the nuclear arms race, and the need to control these awesome weapons. With the factors preventing global cataclysm so precariously balanced, it is only logical that rational people should try to prevent the use of nuclear arms.

The idea of arms control was not new. The Rush-Bagot agreement of 1817 between the United States and England saw the two parties voluntarily limit their opposing naval forces on the Great Lakes. Until the late nineteenth century, however, arms limitations agreements between nations were largely limitations imposed by the victor on the vanquished. Between 1899 and 1907, though, a series of international peace conferences were held at Den Haag (The Hague) that mark some real milestones in the limitation of war and in the settlement of international disputes. The Permanent Court of Arbitration, forerunner of the Permanent Court of International Justice, was established there. Declarations were signed in 1899 prohibiting the use of asphyxiating gases and dumdum bullets, and by 1907 bans on the use of poison and poisoned weapons were adopted, as well as an agreement prohibiting or restricting certain classes of automatic contact mines and torpedoes. The Den Haag conferences were significant as the first major organized efforts of their kind in modern times, but when compared to the great war then looming over Europe they were almost naive.

World War I gave Europe and the world a view of weapons more horrible than anything encountered during the previous history of warfare. From deadly cannons of enormous size to aerial bombs to burning, suffocating poison gas, these weapons made up the fabric of total war, a horrible carnage that pulverized most of Belgium and parts of France. The result was the League of Nations and the Treaty of Versailles, with its unrealistic arms limitations that, imposed on Germany, became the first step in a series of events that led to World War II.

Poison gas was a prime arms control issue following World War I because of the ugly results of its use in that war. In 1925 an agreement was reached in Geneva banning its use, as well as that of bacteriological agents, in warfare. It was signed by all major powers except the United States and Japan. Generally observed by all sides in World War II, it was finally signed by Japan in 1970 and the United States in 1975.

In 1921, the United States initiated a series of conferences directed at curbing the postwar arms race. In those days the arms were battleships and the area of concern was the western Pacific; the parties were the World War I allies with interests in that region—the United States, Britain, and, prophetically, Japan. An agreement was signed that limited warship tonnage and construction of bases and naval fortifications. In 1930 a second treaty was signed in London that expanded the provisions of the first. A third conference was held in 1935, but no agreement was reached, and the earlier treaties expired the following year when Japan refused renewal. A general disarmament conference sponsored by the League of Nations met over the period 1932–1937 with proposals ranging from France's idea for an international police force to a Russian plan promoting complete disarmament. Hitler demanded the right to rearm Germany unless the rest of the world disarmed to Germany's level, and when this did not come about, Hitler withdrew from the conference and the League. Ultimately, the conference, noble in its ideals but short on results, ended without an agreement.

The nuclear weaponry to come out of World War II was many times more gruesome than the poison gas of the First World War and soon seized central importance in disarmament talks. In 1946, Bernard Baruch, who was then the American representative on the United Nations Atomic Energy Commission, suggested that all nuclear weapons be placed under the control of the U.N. The plan was favorably received by most of the members of the U.N., but the Soviet Union, feverishly working toward development of its own nuclear weapons, blocked adoption of the plan. The U.N. continued to address the problem of nuclear weapons and arms control, establishing the U.N. Disarmament Commission in 1952. The U.N. expanded its role in disarmament through a series of larger and larger agencies, the Eighteen Nation Disarmament Committee (1962), the Conference of the Committee on Disarmament (1969), and the Committee on Disarmament, formed in 1978 with forty member states. The United States became the first nation to establish an arms control agency of its own with the creation of the U.S. Arms Control and Disarmament Agency in 1961.

The Soviet Union first expressed interest in achieving some limitation on nuclear weapons testing in May 1955, but the Western powers continued to link this kind of limitation to a broader arms control package. In March 1958 the Soviet Union announced that it would unilaterally suspend nuclear tests and was joined by Britain and the United States in what President Eisenhower would call a "voluntary moratorium." In June 1961 Soviet Premier Khrushchev told President Kennedy in Vienna that the Soviets now considered a test-ban agreement to be linked with general disarmament. In September the Russians resumed nuclear testing, but two months later they announced a willingness to consider negotiating a test-ban with no strings attached. Behind-the-scenes negotiations ensued, both government to government and through the U.N. disarmament committees. Finally, on June 10, 1963, it was announced by the Americans that three-power negotiations would be held in Moscow. Although they had rejected it a year earlier, the Soviets were now willing to exclude underground tests from the talks. The notion of underground tests had been a bone of contention for some time because compliance would be vastly harder to verify than compliance with bans on atmospheric, underwater, or outer space nuclear tests. Without means to verify the compliance of one side by the other, a ban would have no value. Verification of compliance has been, and will continue to be, one of the most important elements of any arms control treaty dealing with any kind of weapon.

When Britain, the United States, and the USSR finally sat down to the table on July 15, many of the details had already been agreed upon behind the scenes, so negotiations moved quickly and smoothly. The Nuclear Test Ban Treaty was initiated on July 25, formally signed at Moscow on August 5, and ratified by President Kennedy on October 7, 1963; it went into force three days later. Under provisions of the treaty, the three parties agreed "to prohibit, to prevent and not to carry out any nuclear weapon test explosion, or any other nuclear explosion, at any place under its jurisdiction or control . . . in the atmosphere; beyond its limits, including outer space; or under water, including territorial waters or high seas; or . . . in any other environment if such explosion causes radioactive debris to be present outside the territorial limits of the State under whose jurisdiction or control such explosion is conducted."

The treaty can be pointed to as a milestone in that all three of the original parties to the treaty have abided by it, and all but one (India) of 133 other signatories have also abided by its provisions. Neither France nor China, the world's other two major nuclear powers, have chosen to sign, however, and the fallout from their atmospheric tests still dusts the wind patterns of the upper atmosphere from time to time.

In the wake of the test ban treaty, the U.N. pressed the nuclear powers for a specific ban on nuclear *weapons* in outer space. On October 17, 1963, the General Assembly unanimously called on the U.S. and the USSR to present a draft treaty. Submitted on June 19, 1966, the Soviet draft called for a ban on nuclear weapons throughout outer space, whereas the American draft, submitted the same day, called for a ban on deployment of nuclear weapons on celestial

Above: President John F. Kennedy signs the Nuclear Test Ban Treaty of 1963. The Treaty banned atomic testing in the atmosphere, outer space and underwater.

bodies. The Americans agreed to the broader scope of the Soviet draft, and a treaty was signed on January 27, 1967; it went into force on October 10 of the same year.

Another treaty, creating a Latin American Nuclear Free Zone was signed on February 14, 1967, and entered into force on April 22, 1968. It is interesting to note that, although the treaty and/or its protocols was signed by nearly all the nations of Latin America (including Argentina, Brazil, and Chile) and the major nuclear powers (including France, China, and the USSR, as well as the U.S. and the United Kingdom), it has never been signed by Cuba.

The next major milestone in the control of nuclear weapons came with the Nuclear Non-Proliferation Treaty. Under its provisions, powers possessing nuclear weapons agree not to transfer nuclear weapons to the control of other powers not possessing them. The Soviet Union was quick to support the treaty in response to Anglo-American plans in the mid-sixties to create a Multilateral Nuclear Force (MLF) or Atlantic Nuclear Force (ANF). As a result of subsequent negotiations, no multination nuclear force was created on either side of the iron curtain, but the United States, Britain, and the USSR were permitted to deploy their nuclear weapons, under their own control, in allied front-line NATO or Warsaw Pact nations. The resulting treaty was signed in July 1968, but ratification by the United States was delayed until March 5, 1970, by the Russian invasion of Czechoslovakia.

Whereas all the earlier treaties dealt with the problems of testing or of the spread of nuclear weapons, it was not until the Strategic Arms Limitation Talks (SALT) that the problem of the ever-growing Soviet and American nuclear arsenals was considered. Proposed at the time of the signing of the Non-Proliferation Treaty, the SALT negotiations finally began in Helsinki on November 17, 1969.

The number of ICBMs under SAC control had been maintained at the 1967 level of 1,054, although the MIRVed Minuteman IIIs were replacing single-warhead missiles within that total. Meanwhile, the Russians had been steadily building up their arsenal. When the SALT talks began, the Russians had about 1,000 ICBMs, but by the time of the SALT I treaty they had surpassed the Americans. The Americans maintained, because of the MIRVs, a lead in terms of the number of warheads, however, and SAC's bomber fleet still outnumbered that of the Russians. Thus, the respective arsenals were described as being, while not necessarily unequal, "asymmetrical."

Arms control negotiations, like any sort of ne-gotiations, can be compared to a parlor game. Each side likes to negotiate from a position of strength and to have the ground rules written to place him in the advantage. So too with the SALT talks. One of the first items on the agenda was a broad-reaching effort to define strategic arms in order to determine which weapons to include in SALT. The United States defined strategic weapons as those with an intercontinental range, that is, weapons that could reach the heart of one nation from the heart of the other. The Soviet negotiators, however, wanted to include weapons of either nation that could strike the other. The Americans opposed this definition because it included medium-range and tactical weapons based in Europe for the defense of NATO countries, which by provision of the Non-Proliferation Treaty had to remain under U.S. control. Russian tactical nuclear weapons would not, under this negotiating scenario, be counted, because they did not have sufficient range to hit the United States. With the two arsenals being asymmetrical, the Russians hoped to add to their intercontinental weaponry by having the American tactical weapons classed as "strategic." The eventual treaty did not address the question; the impasse was sidestepped by a mutual decision to concentrate on achieving a permanent treaty to limit the deployment of anti-ballistic missile (ABM) systems.

Finally, on May 26, 1972, President Nixon and President Brezhnev signed the Treaty on the Limitation of Anti-Ballistic Missile Systems, and the Interim Agreement on Strategic Arms Limitation (SALT I). The ABM treaty permitted each side to develop an ABM system and deploy it at two sites, although a 1974 ABM Protocol later reduced the limit to one each. The sites could have a maximum of 100 interceptor (or anti-missile) missiles at 100 launchers, and the two sites had to be at least 1,300 kilometers apart. The latter provision was to prevent the estab-

Above: Presidents Nixon and Brezhnev sign the SALT I Treaty in Moscow on May 26, 1972.

lishment of a national or regional system of antimissile defense that could trigger a further escalation in the arms race by triggering development of more sophisticated ICBMs or by allowing one side to become reckless, thinking it was immune from attack. The Russians pressed ahead with construction of an ABM field protecting Moscow; the United States had earlier developed the Safeguard ABM system centered near SAC's base at Grand Forks, North Dakota, covering the ICBM fields on the northern Great Plains. The Moscow field became operational in 1980 with ABM-1B interceptor missiles (NATO code name Galosh) based at sixty-four sites.

Work had already begun on the Grand Forks site, but the Safeguard program was terminated still incomplete, and the site has been inoperative since 1969.

The SALT I Interim Agreement was designed as a stopgap measure to accompany the ABM treaty. The idea was to freeze or set limits on the numbers of certain strategic nuclear weapons already in the superpower arsenals and buy time to negotiate a more comprehensive treaty (SALT II). The SALT I treaty accepted the

133

"asymmetry" of the two arsenals and permitted deployment of new ICBMs only by the dismantling of a like number of older systems. Launchers for the older missiles could not be modified to accommodate larger, heavier ICBMs but fixed-site launchers under construction could be completed. The former prevented deployment of the Russians' huge SS–9 heavy ICBM, but the latter permitted them to achieve advantage over SAC in the number of fixed ICBM sites. SALT I counted only fixed and not mobile land-based ICBMs. The Russian point of view was that, because neither side had mobile land-based ICBMs, they should not be included. The American negotiators felt that they should be banned in SALT I but conceded the then-moot point. Subsequently, the Soviets have deployed a mobile IRBM (the SS–20), and the United States has considered a mobile basing system for the MX ICBM.

Under SALT I submarine-launched ballistic missiles (SLBMs) increased on both sides. Under Article III and the protocol, the Soviet navy was allowed to increase its number of launchers from 740 to 950 and the U.S. Navy from 656 (on 41 submarines) to 710 (on 44 subs).

SALT I was signed at a pivotal juncture in the history of strategic nuclear weapons. It was the point at which the Soviet Union surpassed the United States both in the number of strategic weapons delivery systems and in the total megatons of nuclear weapons; it was also the point from which it appeared the superpowers would responsibly address the control of their awesome destructive power. On June 22, 1973, the superpowers signed an Agreement on the Prevention of Nuclear War, in which they stated their perception that "nuclear war would have devastating consequences for mankind . . . [and their] desire to bring about conditions in which the danger of an outbreak of nuclear war anywhere in the world would be reduced and ultimately eliminated . . . the United States and the Union of Soviet Socialist Republics . . . have agreed that an objective of their policies is to remove the danger of nuclear war and of the use of nuclear weapons . . . [and] to proceed from the premise that each Party will refrain from the threat or use of force against the other Party, against the allies of the other Party and against other countries."

SALT I was an interim agreement, and its Article VII called for the two sides to begin negotiations toward a comprehensive long-term treaty to set ceilings on strategic nuclear weapons. The SALT II negotiations got under way in November 1972 and began to take up the issues that had plagued the earlier talks, such as the asymmetry of the two arsenals and the Russian desire to count American tactical nuclear weapons in Europe. Discussions continued for two years, overshadowed by the Watergate crisis in the United States that ultimately brought down Richard Nixon as president. Shortly after assuming the presidency, Gerald Ford met with Russian President Leonid Brezhnev at Vladivostok. During the meeting, the two sides agreed to an *aide-mémoire* that would form the basic framework for SALT II. The Ford administration was short-lived, but the SALT II negotiations were continued by the Carter administration, with almost continuous sessions in Geneva. On June 18, 1979, President Carter and President Brezhnev met in Vienna to sign SALT II, the Treaty on the Limitation of Strategic Offensive Arms. Although SALT II was never ratified by the U.S. Senate, because of the Russian invasion of Afghanistan, both President Carter and President Reagan have stated their intention to abide by its provisions, as have the Soviet leadership.

Among the provisions of SALT II are

- the setting of an equal aggregate limit for the number of delivery systems (ICBMs, SLBMs, bombers, etc.) of 2,400 as agreed in the Vladivostok accords;

- the setting of an equal aggregate limit of 1,320 for launchers of MIRVed ballistic missiles and bombers capable of carrying cruise missiles, with a limit of 820 MIRVed ICBMs;
- a ban on construction of additional ICBM launchers;
- permission for the testing and deployment by each side of only one new ICBM type;
- a ban on expanding the number of warheads in MIRVed missiles, with a limit of ten per new ICBM and fourteen per new SLBM;
- establishment of launch and throw-weight limits;
- a ban on modification of ICBM launchers to handle heavy ICBMs;
- a ban on ICBM launchers that could be rapidly reloaded;
- a ban, because of potential verification problems, on the Soviet SS–16 ICBM, which was similar to the SS–20 and with which it might be confused;
- a ban on new types of strategic weapons that are technically possible but which have not yet been deployed, such as surface-ship-based and ocean-floor-based ballistic missiles;
- agreement for advance notification of specified ICBM test launchings.

SALT II also provided for verification of compliance by what is called "national technical means of verification," which includes the use of strategic reconnaissance and electronic surveillance aircraft and satellites. The treaty also provided for the beginning of further talks (SALT III) in which the two superpowers agreed to "pursue . . . the objectives [of] significant and substantial *reductions* in the numbers of strategic offensive arms; qualitative limitations on strategic offensive arms, including restrictions on the development, testing and deployment of new types of strategic offensive arms and on the modernization of existing strategic offensive arms."

The road leading away from the Carter-Brezhnev embrace at Vienna in the summer of 1979 has been a rocky one. The Russian invasion of Afghanistan at Christmastime half a year later removed Senate ratification of SALT II from the agenda and delayed the SALT III negotiations. The ascendency of the Reagan administration in 1981 brought a new cast of characters to the American side of the bargaining table as well as a new perception both of the talks and of the Russians, now viewed as less than trustworthy. The Reagan perception of arms control took the form in 1981 of a proposal for Strategic Arms Reduction Talks (START), putting the emphasis on a reduction of, rather than the placing of a ceiling on, the superpower arsenals.

As the spring thaw comes to the Swiss Alps and the runoff flows down into Lac Leman and past the Palais des Nations into the Rhone at Geneva, no one can be truly certain of the status of the arms control talks that have watched the coming of two dozen springs to this city. The Russians will dramatically break off the public sessions to make a political point about an unrelated matter, yet private sessions continue. Then they too will break off. Still later, as the chilled clear waters flow down from the mountains, a thaw comes in the bargaining positions. As the debate goes on, the flame of hope that true arms reductions may one day be a reality continues to flicker.

Meanwhile back on the chinook-swept plains of eastern Montana, SAC will remain ready. And the men in the Kremlin will know that, and they will know that between them and world domination stands an organization whose motto is now, as always, Peace Is Our Profession.

Glossary

AAA: Antiaircraft Artillery

AB: Air Base; base used by the USAF outside the continental United States.

ABCCC: Airborne Command and Control Center

ACCS: Automated Command Control System

ACR: Advanced Capability Radar; terrain-following radar.

AD: Air Division

ADVON: Advanced Echelon

AFB: Air Force Base; USAF base within the continental United States.

AFSATCOM: Air Force Satellite Communications System

ALCS: Airborne Launch Control System

ALCM: Air Launched Cruise Missile

AMSA: Advanced Manned Strategic Aircraft

AP: Aerial Refueling Anchor Point

AR: Aerial Refueling

ARCP: Aerial Refueling Control Point

ATB: Advanced Technology Bomber; stealth technology.

C³: Command, Control and Communications

CCPDS: Command Center Processing and Display System

CCCP: Union of Soviet Socialist Republics as abbreviated in Cyrillic alphabet

CINCPAC: Commander in Chief, US Unified Pacific Command

CINSAC: Commander in Chief, Strategic Air Command

DEFCON: Defense Condition; conditions of nuclear alert ranging from normal to order-to-launch.

DSTP: Director of Strategic Target Planning

ECM: Electronic Countermeasures

ERCS: Emergency Rocket Communication System

EW: Electronic Warfare

EWO: Emergency War Order

FEAF: Far East Air Forces, predecessor to PACAF.

FMIS: Force Management Information System

FLIR: Forward Looking Infrared Sensor

GCI: Ground Control Intercept; radar ground control of interceptors.

ICBM: Intercontinental Ballistic Missile

IOC: Initial Operating Capability

IP: Initial Point; beginning of bomb run.

IRAN: Inspect and Repair As Necessary

IRBM: Intermediate Range Ballistic Missile

JSCS: Joint Strategic Connectivity Staff

JCS: Joint Chiefs of Staff

JSTPS: Joint Strategic Target Planning Staff

LLTV: Low Light Television

LRCA: Long Range Combat Aircraft; the original B-1 program.

MACV: Military Assistance Command, Vietnam

MiG: Mikoyan Gurevich; an aircraft design bureau in the USSR and aircraft design by that bureau.

MiGCAP: MiG Combat Air Patrol; US escort fighters protecting other aircraft from MiGs.

MIRV: Multiple Independently Targeted Reentry Vehicles; multiple warhead.

MOB: Main Operating Base

MRBM: Medium Range Ballistic Missile

MX: Missile Experimental

SAC Personnel Strength (In Thousands)

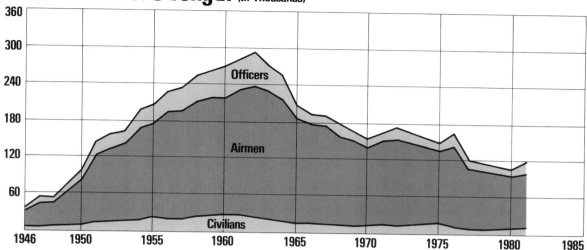

NEACP: National Emergency Airborne Command Post

NCA: National Command Authority

NORAD: North American Air Defense Command

NSTL: National Strategic Target List

OAS: Offensive Avionics System

PACAF: Pacific Air Forces

PACCS: Post Attack Command Control System; to be used after nuclear attack

PAS: Primary Alerting System

POL: Petroleum, oil, lubricants

RDF: Rapid Deployment Force

RN: Radar Navigator; bombardier.

SAC: Strategic Air Command

SACCS: SAC Automated Command Control System

SALT: Strategic Arms Limitation Talks; Strategic Arms Limitation Treaty

SAM: Surface-to-Air Missile

SAR: Search and Rescue

SIOP: Single Integrated Operation Plan

SLBM: Submarine Launched Ballistic Missile

SLFCS: Survivable Low Frequency Communications System

SRAM: Short Range Attack Missile

START: Strategic Arms Reduction Talks

SW: Strategic Wing

SR: Strategic Reconnaissance

SPF: Strategic Projection Force; B-52 units assigned to RDF.

TACAN: Tactical Air Navigation

TDY: Temporary Duty

TERCOM: Terrain Contour Matching

TFR: Terrain Following Radar

TFX: Tactical Fighter, Experimental (original F-111 program)

TF: Task Force

TR: Tactical Reconnaissance

USAAC: United States Army Air Corps; predecessor to the USAF, 1926–1941.

USAAF: United States Army Air Forces; predecessor to the USAF, 1941–1947.

USAAS: United States Army Air Service; predecessor to the USAF, 1918–1926.

USAF: United States Air Force

Acknowledgements

No book on so broad a topic as the Strategic Air Command can be written and produced in a vacuum. During the course of the development of this work I've had the pleasure to work with and receive assistance from a number of individuals whose contributions deserve mention. First of all, there is Mrs. Alice Price of the Air Force Art and Museum Branch, without whom I never would have found myself looking at the Idaho and Nevada badlands from 500 feet through the cockpit of Major MacTaggert's 93d Bomb Wing B–52, and without whom none of this would have been possible. For background information, thanks are due to Lt. Col. Richard L. Kline of SAC Headquarters at Offutt AFB (who supplied much valuable information on Line-backer II) and Airman First Class Robert H. Craig of the First Strategic Aerospace Division at Vandenberg AFB. For assistance in assembling the photographs I'd like to thank Marilyn Phipps of Boeing Historical Services, Richard Stadler of Lockheed, Dana Bell at the National Air and Space Museum, Lt. Col. Eric Solander of the Air Force Office of Public Affairs, and especially 1st Lt. Peter Meltzer, Jr., of the latter office. Thanks are also due to S. R. Elliot of the International Institute of Strategic Studies in London and M. Sgt. Roger Jernigan of the Office of Air Force History, who is always able to provide even the most obscure bits of information. Finally, a special thanks to Rod Baird for his indispensable assistance in the design and cartography of this book and all those that preceded it; and to Carol Yenne, without whose nimble fingers on the keyboard of a borrowed Selectric there would have been no manuscript.

About the Author:

Bill Yenne is a San Francisco-based book designer and life-long aviation enthusiast whose association with the US Air Force began in 1978 when he first supplied paintings for the Official Air Force collection. Since then, he has done more than a dozen paintings for the collection, including one that hangs in the Chief of Staff's dining room.

He is also a member of the Air Force Association and the American Aviation Historical Society.

As a writer specializing in aviation history, his previous books include *Boeing: Planemaker to the World; McDonnell Douglas: A Tale of Two Giants; The History of the US Air Force; The Encyclopedia of US Spacecraft* and *German War Art, 1939-1945*.

(Photo by Robert Bausch)